WILDERNESS WALKS

Photographs by Colin Prior

WILDERNESS
WALKS

Cameron McNeish and Richard Else

BBC BOOKS

This book is published to accompany the television series entitled *Wilderness Walks* which was first broadcast in 1997. The series was produced by Triple Echo Productions Ltd.
Executive Producer: Ken MacQuarrie
Producer-director: Richard Else

Published by BBC Books,
an imprint of BBC Worldwide Publishing,
BBC Worldwide Limited, Woodlands,
80 Wood Lane, London W12 0TT

First published 1997
© Richard Else and Cameron McNeish 1997
The moral right of the authors has been asserted.

ISBN 0 563 37176 5

Maps by Chris Shaw
Photographs by Colin Prior

Designed by BBC Books
Set in Goudy
Printed and bound in Great Britain by Butler & Tanner, Frome and London
Colour separations by Radstock Reproductions Ltd
Jacket printed by Lawrence Allen Ltd, Weston-super-Mare

Previous Page: Rannoch Moor and the Blackmount Deer Forest

Contents

Preface

This book, and the television series that it accompanies, go back a long way. We both hope it is more than a simple guide to where to place your feet. Our thanks go to the following people without whom the book and television series would have been impossible. Firstly, to Ken MacQuarrie and Colin Cameron at BBC Scotland for once again showing such enthusiasm and commitment for our enterprise. At BBC Books our thanks are due to editors Suzanne Webber, Martha Caute and Khadija Manjlai for not simply their support, but also for their understanding when walking and writing were in competition with each other! At the offices of Triple Echo Productions David Taylor and Laura Hill have shown a similar patience and have made sure the films were coherent when weather and many other factors conspired to produce the opposite effect. Naturally we are delighted that Colin Prior has been able to contribute such memorable panoramic photographs. For someone who is happy to produce just one image a day if the weather permits (and it often doesn't), this is a remarkable achievement for which we are grateful. We are also most grateful to Berghaus, Lowe Alpine, Terra Nova Tents and Moutain Equipment for allowing us the use of their products whilst we were working on this book.

Margaret Wicks has again corrected the wayward personalities of both writers to ensure that deadlines were met, proofs checked, photographs agreed and the hundred and one tasks that surround authorship performed. Without her constant encouragement and chivvying, this book would still be trapped somewhere inside our personal computers!

Finally, but by no means last, we wanted to thank the guests who took part in the BBC films, for sharing their insights into the Scottish wilderness and its importance.

Whilst we hope there are no errors of substance in these pages, do bear in mind that bus, train and ferry timetables can alter, as can the hospitality provided by hotels and pubs.

Cameron McNeish and Richard Else

INTRODUCTION

•

Cameron McNeish

Back-to-back sixty-metre sprints represent a form of athletics torture. The distance isn't the problem – most folk with even a tad of fitness can sprint for sixty metres; the difficulties arise when you get only ten seconds in which to recover. That's barely time to turn around and get back to the start. The idea is to make as many runs as you can until you fail to make the distance.

It was the late 1960s and I was in exalted company: David Jenkins, who was to go on to win a European championship at 400 metres, Stewart McCallum, Scottish decathlon champion, and Duncan Middleton, British indoors 800-metre champion. Working out close by was a gangly youth by the name of Alan Wells. Alan, who was later to become Olympic 100-metre gold medallist, was a long jumper in those days, like me. I was Scottish junior champion and had represented the Scottish Amateur Athletic Association in a couple of international events. The Commonwealth Games were coming up, and I was in the pool of athletes from which the Scottish team would be selected. In the eyes of most folk my star was well and truly on the ascendancy – but I was unsettled and dissatisfied with my lot.

As I staggered from the track after several lung-bursting runs, with every lactic acid-laden limb throbbing and crying out for rest, my gaze would involuntarily drift up from the track in the Meadowbank Stadium in Edinburgh towards Arthur's Seat, the ancient volcano which dominates that lovely city. I knew that up there skylarks would be singing, there would be people wandering over the high slopes, looking across the Firth of Forth to the hills of Fife and beyond, to the distant blue outline of the Highlands, and that's where I wanted to be.

At the age of nineteen I was in mental turmoil. I was passionate about athletics. I loved the achievement, the discipline, the competition and the camaraderie of my team mates. I wanted my success to reflect the dedication and commitment of my coaches, John Anderson and Frank Dick, two men who had invested so much time on me over the years. But I also loved the hills – the scale and the grandeur, the elemental touch of rock and the feel of the wind, the far-flung view and the simple blend of fresh air and freedom.

I had been walking and climbing, off and on, for several years. At the age of fourteen, on a family outing to Glen Coe, I had experienced a strange little incident which had a powerful influence on me at the time. We had stopped in a lay-by, and on the hill above the road I had glimpsed movement and saw two men scramble down from the crags high above the glen. They were suntanned and lean, and one of them had a coiled rope over his shoulder. They wore tartan shirts, corduroy breeches and big Alpine boots and as they crossed the rough, rocky ground their movement was relaxed and easy. It was apparent, even to my inexperienced eyes, that they were completely at home in that wild environment. I've no idea who they were, but on that sunny day they could have been Fianna warriors, heroes of the legendary Ossianic tales, returning from Tir nan Og, the Land of the Ever Young; they could have been gods descending from Olympus. They were just climbers, returning from a day in the mountains, but to my young eyes they symbolized exactly what I wanted to be.

As I watched them disappear beyond our car I made a promise to myself: one day I was going to be one of them.

Ultimately, I had to decide between track and field and the wider horizons of the mountains. I had joined the City of Glasgow Police Force straight from school, initially as a police cadet and then as a cop pounding the beat in Govan, an area of the city where I had been born, and it was on a trip with the Police Hill Walking Club that eventually I made the decision which was to change my life. It was a sun-soaked day on the Isle of Arran and, with another policeman, Arnott Faichney, I had traversed those wonderful craggy ridges, over Beinn Tarsuinn and the A' Chir Ridge, over the Witch's Step towards Goat Fell.

We had spent too long on the sun-kissed granite and had to run down the hill to catch our bus back to the ferry at Brodick. As we loped down the hillside, exhilarated by our achievements on the narrow, exposed ridges, I suddenly remembered those two men I had seen years before in Glen Coe. Intoxicated by the movement, by the surroundings, by the sheer beauty of the place, I was aware immediately that I had, at last, become one of them. It was something I couldn't risk losing.

It was years later that I read these words by Henry David Thoreau, and I knew straight away that they reflected my decision that day on Arran: 'I went to the woods because I wished to live deliberately, to front only the essential facts of life, and see if I could not learn what it had to teach, and not, when I came to die, discover that I had not lived.'

But I didn't want to live 'deliberately' only at weekends and holidays. I wanted to immerse myself totally and completely in the mountains and wild places, to work in the hills and to live in the hills. Chris Bonington's autobiography, I Chose to Climb, had a profound influence on me at the time. In that book he describes a series of failures in his life – school, his army career, his job as a margarine salesman – until at the age of thirty or so he gave it all up, moved to the Lake District and tried to earn a living as a professional mountaineer.

I admired his persistence, his ambition and his single-minded determination to succeed, but Chris was a well-known and successful climber. He had climbed the North Face of the Eiger, for goodness sake! Compared to Chris I was a mere clamberer and bumbler. While I loved climbing, my real motivation was taking off for several days at a time, wandering the hills with all my needs in a rucksack on my back. I was a back-packer, and backpackers rarely made headline news in the world's press, with glossy magazines wanting you to write for them.

But I was fortunate. I moved to the Highlands and wrote and took photographs. More recently I've made radio and television programmes, and for twenty years have lived in the very shadow of the Cairngorms. I've been fortunate – indeed lucky – but such fortune is never without sacrifice. The great violinist Fritz Kreisler once met a lady who said to him, 'Mr Kreisler, I would give my life to play the violin like you do.'

'Madam,' the musician replied, 'I did.'

And while I have given much of my life to this odd career which is dominated by mountains and wild places, I'm also aware that for most folk these are experiences which can be, and are, enjoyed and appreciated at weekends and during holidays.

For most folk, Thoreau's 'woods' offer a place in which to experience the natural world, a world of mountains, rivers, forests and flowers. Woods or wilderness, wild land or the 'green world', the nomenclature is unimportant; the vital issue is that within that world we can enjoy the peace and the beauty, the space and the silence, far away from the stresses and problems of everyday life.

Throughout the quarter-century since I made that decision about my future, I've enjoyed such places not only in my native Scotland but throughout the world – the Alps, the Arctic, the Himalayas, the Caucasus, the Pyrenees and Africa. And it's note-worthy that I have never been disappointed in any of the mountains I have climbed or walked over. I would suggest that this is because wild places transcend political and nationalist boundaries – wilderness has a deeper significance not only for those who seek recreation but for mankind itself.

I rock-climb, climb snow and ice in winter, I ski-tour, I ride a mountain bike and I canoe. But predominantly I walk, with passion and relish, as often as I possibly can.

Wilderness backpacking is exposing yourself to the 'green world' with respect, mini-mizing your impact on it, treating it on its own terms and not trying to urbanize it, walking for several days, or weeks, carrying in a pack on your back everything you need for survival. It does not rely on porters or animals carrying your gear; nor does it rely on engines or wheels. Having said that, wilderness backpacking involves – probably hypocritically but to a degree that the individual backpacker can choose – a dependence on technology.

Our lightweight camping stoves are infinitely more efficient and less environmen-tally damaging than a camp-fire. Our rucksacks and tents are a triumph of design and technology. Our boot-soles are made of rubber, we wear on our backs the latest in poly-tetrafluoroethylene, a chemical shield against the elements, and we salve our green consciences by wearing fleece jackets recycled from plastic bottles. While double standards certainly exist, the eco-gear movement is gaining ground, and more equipment manufacturing companies are recycling fabrics and materials – as well as cash, for it's encouraging that the more visionary companies are putting an environmental royalty on the price of their gear which is then recycled into conservation work, footpath maintenance and the purchase of important wilderness areas for the nation.

The Brasher Boot Company, for example, through the Brasher Trust, has donated hundreds of thousands of pounds to organizations like the National Trust and the John Muir Trust to help buy places like West Affric in Wester Ross, Blà Bheinn and Chlas Glas on the Isle of Skye, Ladhar Bheinn in Knoydart and the splendid Sandwood Bay in Sutherland. The fact that all these places are in the Highlands and Islands of Scotland suggests that it's within those areas that our finest wild land exists.

It's therefore no accident that the walks in this book are in the Highlands and Islands of Scotland, and for that we make no apology. In terms of the deeper philosophy of wilderness appreciation, these walks could be in any wild areas of the world – the values are the same; the space, the grandeur, the natural beauty, the lack of people… But in terms of wilderness backpacking the walks are all short. The distance has been determined largely by the size of the land – in world terms we live on a very small island, and what is encouraging is that so much of this tiny island is wild land.

The choice of walks has been influenced by what wild land means to Richard and myself. I like to get up high in the mountains, to enjoy the far-flung view and the wide open skies, weaving a rather loose and desultory route over the Munros. In 1991, the centenary of the publication of *Munro's Tables*, the official list of all these mountains, I climbed Ben More on Mull, my last Munro. The climbing of them all was a fairly relaxed effort over twenty-five years, and now, for no better reason than 'why not', I'm climbing them all again – hence the visits to the Blackmount, around Loch Mullardoch, through Knoydart, and over the high tops of the Cairngorms. I'm also intrigued by solitude, and the loneliness and mystery of the Minigaig route have helped me to explore some of the more esoteric reasons of why we want to experience wilderness.

Richard has chosen five walks that reflect his interest in the Scottish wilderness, and while he is also keen to be on the high tops he admits to a concern that the recent rise in interest in Munro-bagging is in danger of turning into an obsession that excludes much of our wilderness and a true enjoyment of it. This applies especially to the walks on Mull and Harris – so if you are suffering from a terminal dose of Munro-itis then these superb walks could be the first step to your recovery!

Access – the Scottish dimension

All the land we've written about is owned by someone, and the current law of the land expects us to respect that fact. It has always been understood that in Scotland the hill-goer, mountaineer or backpacker has enjoyed a moral right to roam in wild places, provided he or she exercises good countryside manners and respect for other activities also carried out in these wild areas, such as deerstalking and grouse-shooting.

The law in Scotland at present specifies that a trespass has been committed by a person who goes on to land owned or occupied by another without that person's consent and without having a right to do so. But this is not enshrined in statute as a criminal offence, so there cannot be a prosecution. The owner or occupier must either obtain an interdict or, if damage to property has occurred, raise an action for damages. Additionally, a 'trespasser' may be asked by the owner or occupier to leave the property and, in the event of that person refusing, the owner or occupier has the right to use 'reasonable force' to make him or her leave. There is no further definition of reasonable force. The Criminal Justice Act 1995 makes 'aggravated access' a criminal act, but the landowner or his agent must be able to prove that the person has come on to the land with the deliberate intention of disrupting the lawful activity of the estate.

Having said all that, both public and landowners widely accept that walkers, climbers and backpackers are more or less free to roam the upland areas of the Scottish Highlands without undue restriction.

Most estates in the Highlands and Islands are involved in deerstalking and ask hill-goers to respect the stag-shooting season, which generally runs from 20 August to 20 October. Often a chat with the keeper or factor can tell you where shooting will be taking place. Sometimes a keeper can tell you of a better route than the one you've planned. Bear in mind that although many people disagree with the whole concept of hunting and shooting, such sport does exist and many estates claim to earn a large part of their annual income from stalking. The alternative, however much we may feel disinclined towards such blood sports, could well be something considerably more unpleasant, like mass coniferization.

Mountain Safety

Appropriate safety precautions must always be taken when venturing on to the Scottish hills. Don't set off without waterproofs and spare clothing, even in summer, and food, a map, compass, whistle and torch are vital items of equipment. Conditions in winter are often Arctic in nature and just as severe as those on higher European mountains. Such conditions must be treated with respect; an ice-axe, crampons and specialist winter gear are essential, as is an understanding of snow conditions, including avalanches and cornices. Everyone venturing on to the Scottish hills in winter should be able to navigate accurately, especially as the weather changes extremely abruptly. Remember that there is no such thing as winter hill-walking – in the normal conditions of a Scottish winter the activity is no less than mountaineering – so if you don't feel competent as a mountaineer, stay low down. Even better, enrol with one of the Scottish climbing courses which are offered by numerous qualified instructors and organizations in the Highlands.

And when you do finally set off on your wilderness discovery trip, let someone know where you are going and when you will return. Every year search-parties waste countless hours looking for people in the wrong places. The appreciation of our wild lands is heightened by the peace of mind that comes with knowing that if something should go drastically wrong, at least the rescue teams will know where to look for you.

The Munro Game

In 1890 a soldier and diplomat by the name of Sir Hugh Munro, of Lindertis in Angus, compiled a list of the 3000-foot (914-m) mountains in Scotland. In the list, published in the *Scottish Mountaineering Club Journal* in 1891, he claimed that 538 tops were over 3000 feet, 283 of which he believed merited status as 'separate mountains'. (There has always been much speculation about the criteria for deciding what separates a 'top' from a 'mountain'. In 1933, J. Gall Inglis, then editor of *Munro's Tables*, suggested that there should be a drop of 75–100 feet (23–31 m) between mountains, but to date there has been no firm guideline on what constitutes a 'mountain'. Munro himself was in favour of updating only when maps were re-surveyed and revised.)

Almost as soon as Munro had published his first list, the Ordnance Survey published its revised six-inch maps of Scotland and obvious discrepancies were found in Munro's tabulations. Immediately, he began revising his tables but sadly died in 1919, aged sixty-three, before they were published. J.R. Young and A.W. Peacock, fellow-members of the SMC, took on the task and, working from Munro's notes, produced revised tables in 1921. Since then, following various OS surveys and revisions of the tables, the number of 'official' Munros has settled at 277.

In recent years it has become almost fashionable to take up Munro-bagging, attempting to climb all 277 mountains. Some folk take a lifetime to achieve the round; others take on the challenge as a major expedition of a lifetime and climb them all in three or four months. To date the Munros have been climbed in fifty-one days (the fastest), during the months of the Winter equinox (Martin Moran in 1984–5), and with a mountain bike!

The Scottish Mountaineering Club keeps a list of all those who have 'compleated' (*sic*) the round of Munros. The present 'keeper' of those records is Dr C.M. Huntley, Old Medwyn, Spittal, Carnwath, Lanarkshire ML11 8LY. At the time of writing there are about 1500 Munroists on the list. Taken on trust, you simply write a letter to the SMC to inform it of your 'completion'; you then appear on the honours list.

While the Munros comprise 277 Scottish mountains that lift their heads over the 3000-foot contour, the Corbetts, named after John Rooke Corbett, make up another 221 separate hills over 2500 feet (764 m) scattered throughout the Highlands and Islands.

CHAPTER ONE

KNOYDART

A MAN-MADE WILDERNESS

•

Cameron McNeish

A three-day walk across the peninsula of Knoydart from Kinloch Hourn to Inverie via Barrisdale, Ladhar Bheinn, Luinne Bheinn and Meall Buidhe

---

MAP: *OS 1:50 000 Sheet 33*

START: *Kinloch Hourn. Grid Ref: 950066*

FINISH: *Inverie. Grid Ref: 766999*

LENGTH: *24 miles (39 km)*

APPROXIMATE TIME: *2–3 days*

TERRAIN: *Mixed. Easy path and track walking for much of the way, but the mountains are remote and virtually trackless*

ACCOMMODATION: *No accommodation at Kinloch Hourn although the Tomdoun Hotel in Glen Garry can be recommended. The Barrisdale Estate operates a private bothy and basic camping area at Barrisdale (small overnight charge, but they at least supply toilet paper in the lavatory). There is guest-house and b&b accommodation, plus a good restaurant, at Inverie. The Forge Inn at Inverie, the most remote pub on the mainland according to The Guinness Book of Records, is a good place for crack (friendly chat), occasional music and good beer. There is also excellent bunkhouse and chalet accommodation at Doune Marine (reference GR703036) at the westernmost point of the peninsula; more information from Mary Robinson on (01687) 2667*

I f you take the people away from a land, from places where generations have worked and toiled to earn a living from ground uncompromising in its difficulty, that land will, in no time at all, reassert its hold. Bracken fronds will eagerly swallow up the lazy beds, old run rigs will fade into mere tracings, and green and ochre lichens will creep over the ruckles of stone which once housed families and their cattle.

It's strange how things change, and how modern perceptions can be so different from reality. The peninsula of Knoydart, jutting out into the Sound of Sleat with all the character of an island, is generally perceived to be a wilderness. When the MoD wanted to buy it at the end of the 1980s there was public outcry. 'Scotland's last

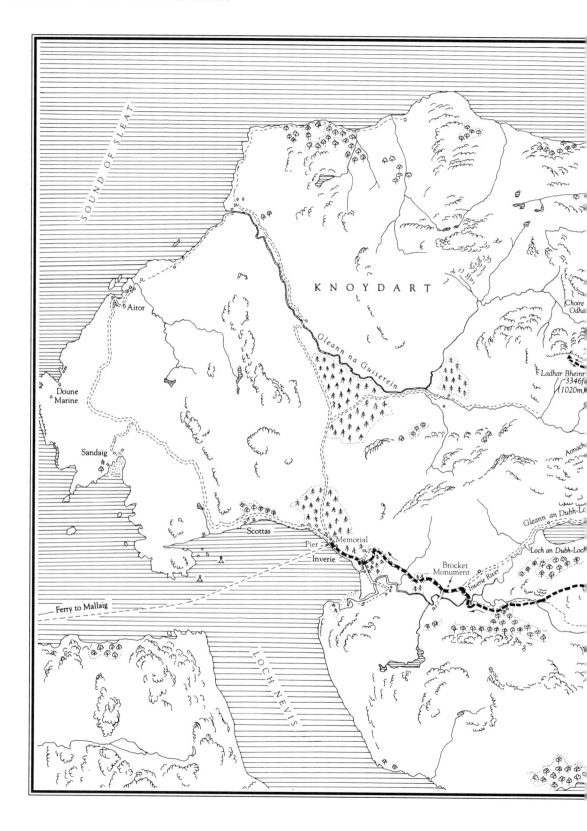

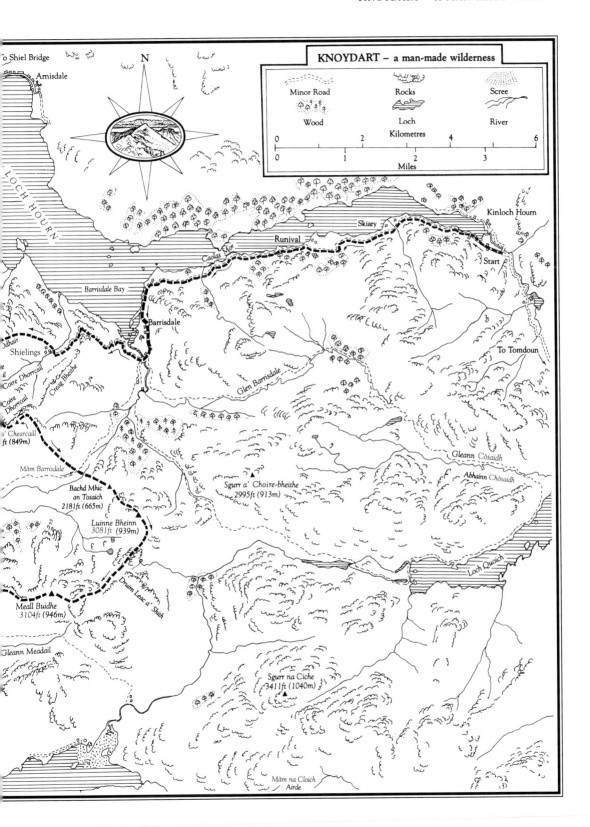

KNOYDART – a man-made wilderness

Minor Road   Rocks   Scree

Wood   Loch   River

Kilometres
0   2   4   6

Miles
0   1   2   3

N

To Shiel Bridge
Arnisdale

LOCH HOURN

Kinloch Hourn
Skiary
Runival
Caolas Mòr
Start

Barrisdale Bay

Barrisdale

To Tomdoun

Shielings

Coire Dhorrcail
Creag Bheithe

Glen Barrisdale

Gleann Còsaidh

Coire Dhorrcail

a' Chearcaill
ft (849m)

Màm Barrisdale

Abhainn Chòsaidh

Sgurr a' Choire-bheithe
2995ft (913m)

Bachd Mhic
an Tosaich
2181ft (665m)

Luinne Bheinn
3081ft (939m)

Loch Quoich

Druim Leac a' Shìth

Meall Buidhe
3104ft (946m)

Gleann Meadail

Sgurr na Ciche
3411ft (1040m)

Màm na Cloich
Airde

wilderness,' said the press proclamations. And yet Knoydart is, and always was, less of a natural wilderness than the Cairngorms, Torridon, the Cuillin, Inverpollaidh, the Fannichs, the Blackmount and many other mountain areas of Scotland. This is no savage or untamed land.

Just after the 1745 rebellion, over a thousand young men, the clans fighting force, worked the land, paying what was known as 'warrior rent'. Townships were sizeable in places like Skiary and Barrisdale, Doune, Airor and Glenguiserain, Sandaig and Inverie. Even inland, in Gleann an Dubh-Lochain and Gleann Meadail, farmlands grew grain and potatoes, and an etching from the last century clearly shows forty to fifty trading ships at anchor in Barrisdale Bay.

But the townships have gone. Today, Inverie is the only real modern settlement, with a pier, a cluster of whitewashed cottages, a pub and a guest-house. Despite its small size, Inverie is very much the focal centre of the peninsula, with a very strong community spirit. After several changes in land ownership in Knoydart, there is currently a desire among the local folk to own the land themselves. Stretching out westwards from those rugged mountains which form the romantic-sounding Rough Bounds of Knoydart, the peninsula is sequestered from the rest of the mainland by long, winding sea lochs. Common belief suggests that Loch Nevis and Loch Hourn are corruptions of the Gaelic words for 'heaven' and 'hell', placing Knoydart in some sort of montane limbo.

Choice of access is limited – a long walk from Kinloch Hourn in the north or from Glen Dessarry via the Màm na Cloich Airde in the south, or ferry from Mallaig or Arnisdale, the latter being the keeper's rowing-boat. Perhaps it's no small wonder that people regard Knoydart as being as remote as anywhere you will find on the mainland.

Bill Murray, possibly Scotland's greatest-ever mountaineering and landscape writer, described Knoydart thus: 'These numerous glens and tracks, free from all motor traffic, give excellent walking through wild country. They breathe a peace that other areas lack, they have a remoteness without desolation, and a beauty without blemish.' On the contrary, the late Seton Gordon, that marvellous old sennachie (storyteller) of the wild places, had described it as: 'A wild country of dark sea lochs and gloomy hills, often mist shrouded. Here the clans of the uruisgean, or spectres, must roam, here the each uisge and the tarbh uisge, the water bulls, perhaps fight fierce battles. I do not think the daoine sith, the hill faeries, are here. The country is too vast and forbidding for the Little People.'

A beauty without blemish, or vast and forbidding? I've known Knoydart wear both guises. I've festered in the sun high on Luinne Bheinn and Ladhar Bheinn, soaking up the breathtaking beauty of the place, and I've struggled over the high Màm Barrisdale in drifting snow, the surrounding hills swathed in cloaks of grey. Knoydart can be a place of contrasts.

Kinloch Hourn to Barrisdale

•

The landscape was far from forbidding as David Craig and I shouldered our packs at Kinloch Hourn, intent on a good three-day romp over the peninsula. David, an Aberdonian by birth, is Professor of Creative Writing at Lancaster University and is one of the most enthusiastic climbers I have ever known. He is also a poet, a characteristic immediately evident in his conversation as he exclaimed his delight at his surroundings – the salt-flats at the head of the loch, the views of the 'back' of the Saddle and Sgurr na Sgine, and the sound of our first cuckoo of the year. Spring had arrived at Kinloch Hourn.

Our plan was a simple one: to take the shoreline footpath for six miles to Barrisdale, where we would camp for the night before climbing Ladhar Bheinn, the most westerly of the mainland Munros. From there we would descend to Màm Barrisdale, the high pass that crosses the spine of the land, and hopefully climb Luinne Bheinn and Meall Buidhe, before dropping down to Inverie, where we would head for Doune on the west coast. Here, some old friends of mine, the Robinsons, were organizing a ceilidh for us. That was a good incentive not to tarry too long on the hills.

But this was, for me, more than just another wilderness walk. David Craig is also the author of the book *On the Crofters' Trail*, a highly acclaimed account of the effects of the Highland Clearances and I wanted to learn more about this awful period in Scotland's history. David's interest in things historical, and indeed in all things Scottish, stemmed from a childhood spent wandering around the castles of the north-east with his uncle, the noted historian and writer Douglas Simpson.

David had come to understand that for a long, dark period in Scotland's history many of her people were evicted from their homes, the homes that had been their fathers' and their grandfathers' before them, forcibly evicted by landowners, many of whom a few years earlier had been their clan chiefs, patriarchal figures in a community system which dominated the Highlands and Islands. In researching his book, he travelled through twenty-one islands in both Scotland and Canada searching out the memories of the descendants of those forced to leave Scotland by the Clearances. This oral tradition was important to him, and I was keen to hear his observations on what he claimed was ethnic cleansing.

With the few buildings of Kinloch Hourn behind us and the pull of the west in front, we talked of the emptiness of the land, this man-made wilderness – not only in Knoydart, but throughout the Highlands and Islands.

'The emptiness is there,' David remarked. 'Strath Brora is empty, and Kildonan and Ousdale and Strath Halladale and Aberscross, and Strath Naver above all. Until the Countess of Sutherland's gangs came with their writs and torches in 1814 and 1819

ABOVE: LOOKING ACROSS LOCH HOURN NEAR THE START OF THE WALK TOWARDS THE HILLS OF GLEN SHIEL. LOCH HOURN HAS BEEN DESCRIBED AS THE GRANDEST OF THE FISSURES WHICH TEAR INTO SCOTLAND'S WEST COAST.

LEFT: CAMERON MCNEISH AND DAVID CRAIG ON LADHAR BHEINN, HIGH ABOVE LOCH HOURN.

•

there were clachans all along Strath Naver: 64 townships housed 338 families. It is one of the old sites of civilization in Britain – its population peak was probably reached in the Bronze Age – it could have a civilization again. Instead, for 150 years it has had masters of fox-hounds from the Home Counties who go up there to fish and shoot, owners of airlines, princes, the head of the Liverpool Cotton Exchange, who made a fortune selling khaki for use in Passchendaele and Vimy, lords-lieutenants of various shires, and their friends, loitering heirs of City directors.'

His dislike for the gentry was undisguised and he told me of his first encounter with a landowner, as a youngster stravaiging (wandering) the length of the western seaboard during long holidays. 'I'll always remember it,' he said, 'this walking Harris tweed cocking a finger at me. 'We are shooting on *my* hill today; you can't go there,' came the clipped tones. 'It seems weird to me,' remarked the young Craig, 'that anyone can own a mountain, or own a river, or own a moor.' The landowner turned out to be no less than Sir Hereward Wake, who instantly condemned David as being a communist, and, 'drove off in a thick blue cloud of high dudgeon'.

Chuckling at the thought of it, we had to get on with the business of tramping the miles to Barrisdale, where we intended camping for the night. But that was no burdensome task. In the late-afternoon sun the loch sparkled with a blue intensity which contrasted richly with the dun, winter-parched colour of the shores. Cinching up our packs, we tramped over seaweed covered tracks, sweated up the long and rocky incline out of Skiary and wondered at the glory of the west pulling us onwards from beyond the pointed silhouette of Ladhar Bheinn. All around us came the cry of gulls, the loon-like cry of the herring gull in particular, an exulting *kaaaa-reeee*, which always evokes in me a strange feeling. It's the sound of mindless wastes of water, the cry of a soul which is not a soul; weird, lost, doomed, and yet, strangely, totally triumphant. A cry of invincible wildness!

In many ways it matched the reputation of Loch Hourn, which has been described as the grandest of the fissures which tear into Scotland's west coast. Reaching far and deep inland from the Sound of Sleat to the high ground of Loch Quoich, it winds tortuously into the heart of the country, more like a great Norwegian fiord. Seton Gordon compares it to a lake of the infernal regions, and the comparison is not at all fanciful. Indeed, Loch Hourn has an aura of mystique acquired through Gaelic mythology as the ancestral home of Domhnull Dubh, the devil. One school of thought suggests that Hourn is a corruption of Iutharn, which means 'hell'! Interestingly, David felt that the name was possibly Norse, meaning 'horn', which could perhaps be corroborated by the curving sweep of the loch. We argued about it for several miles in a light-hearted banter.

The wild waters of Loch Hourn appear more benign at Barrisdale than anywhere else in its whole length, the white shores clean and bright, and the small islands emerald green. It was a peaceful scene, but times weren't always so quiet. The Barrisdale Macdonnells were 'out' with Dundee at the Battle of Killiecrankie, and later fought under the banner of Glengarry at the Battle of Sheriffmuir during the first of the Jacobite rebellions.

After the '45, a long-drawn-out period of emigration from Knoydart began. A combination of potato blights and the failure of the migrating herring shoals brought famine and dire poverty to the area. The chief at the time, Aeneas of Glengarry, sold all his lands except Knoydart and sailed to Australia, only to return in 1852 to die at Inverie. After his death, his widow, Josephine Macdonnell along with her factor, one Alexander Grant, began clearing the remaining tenants to make way for sheep. Four hundred people were evicted, their homes torn down around them, and they were hounded like animals on to the *Sillary*, the transport ship supplied by the British government.

I could visualize the destitute, the women keening loudly, the men hirpling along (slowly dragging their feet) under the weight of their possessions. A contemporary report by *The Times* described the pathos of the scene. 'So long as there was hope of being left with a covering over their heads, the cottars were comparatively quiet, but now that they were homeless many of them became frantic with grief, and were driven to seek shelter in some of the neighbouring quarries, where some are now living, and others among the caves of the rocks with which this wild district of the Highlands abounds.'

The report concluded with the prophetic remark: 'It is thus clear that the Highlands will all become sheepwalks and shooting grounds before long.'

By this time we had dropped down towards Barrisdale Bay, past the roofless walls that were once the community church. It's a magnificent position. Across the bay, Ladhar Bheinn rears up in Alpine glory, its notched and toothed outline above Coire Dhorrcail rising to a single snow-corniced summit. Further down the loch, the blue outline of Skye's Sleat peninsula fills the horizon.

In front of us, a narrow tidal promontory reached out to a small green islet, where the gravestones of some of the evicted form a sad testimony to the harshness of man. We walked out to it, in the sharp early-evening light, remembering those who had to leave a land they loved, their homeland, for an unknown future. David painted a poetic word-picture of the ship easing its way out of the sea loch, the tear-stained faces of the emigrants silently bidding farewell as the sound of the pipes echoed around the now empty hillsides.

I wanted to cry.

Mere flakes of stone, some standing, some flat – no inscriptions recalling the names of the dead, no epitaphs telling of their hardships, only the distant crooning of eider ducks portraying any sense of pibroch lament, an evocative and ghostly sound. We talked of the evictors and the evicted, of the sheep and the flockmasters from the south, who quickly realized that it would pay them to hire ships to remove all those who stood in their way. And it was with a sense of guilt that we concluded eventually

ABOVE: THE SIX-MILE WALK ALONG THE SOUTH SHORE OF LOCH HOURN BETWEEN KINLOCH HOURN AND
BARRISDALE IS MUCH MORE THAN JUST A 'LONG WALK IN'. THE SCENERY IS DRAMATIC AND IT'S WORTH
REMEMBERING THAT THE GREAT SCOTTISH WRITER SETON GORDON COMPARED LOCH HOURN TO A 'LAKE OF
THE INFERNAL REGIONS'.

RIGHT: LADHAR BHEINN FROM THE BARRISDALE PATH IN EARLY FEBRUARY. THE MOST WESTERLY MUNRO ON
THE SCOTTISH MAINLAND, THE SUMMIT RISES TO THE RIGHT OF THE GREAT HOLLOW
OF COIRE DHORRCAIL.

•

that what we have left is a land emptied of people, in which we can enjoy our passion – the enjoyment of wilderness, even if it is a man-made wilderness, created at such a terrible cost.

We camped outside the Barrisdale Bothy. I had been in contact with one of the owners of the estate, Robert Gordon, who quickly had robbed me of any notion of a wilderness experience. In the previous nine months he estimated that over 2500 came to Barrisdale – a number of day-visitors by boat from Arnisdale, but most by way of the footpath from Kinloch Hourn. A retired schoolteacher living at Runival has been given the task of maintaining the path in return for rent.

Gordon and his brothers have seen many changes to Barrisdale even in their time. Once, he said, every small pool had a salmon in it, but now even the loch is empty. In his words, it has been raped. Now just the cockles are left, and the thousands of oyster-catchers they remember from their childhood have virtually vanished. He told me that the one fisherman who makes a living in the bay should not really be fishing, but on the other hand it's a job, and employment is vital.

Barrisdale to Ladhar Bheinn

•

We talked of these things the next morning as we tramped up the zigzag path over into Coire Dhorrcail, of the hoovering up of the ocean-bed by the great factory ships, the damage done by the eternally chomping teeth of sheep and deer, the efforts at conserving fragments of our wild places while we slowly poison our whole planet – thoughts at one with the rain which swept down in sheets from a leaden sky.

I asked David about his communism. He said that he couldn't be a communist now, without a party – he was probably a communist by inclination. My own simple assessment was that his brand of socialism seemed closer to Christianity than Marxism, and that he, self-confessed atheist as he may be, was probably closer to spiritual truths than is some of the dogma issued by the contemporary Christian Church. Curiously, he didn't argue that one, and that was maybe just as well for the zigzags were opening out as we breasted the brow of Creag Bheithe and dropped down into the splendour of Coire Dhorrcail.

This side of Ladhar Bheinn is owned by the John Muir Trust, which bought it a number of years ago after the threatened purchase of Knoydart by the MoD fell through. This organization is named after the pioneering conservationist who as a child moved from Dunbar in East Lothian to America and later became the father-figure of the American National Parks. Now the John Muir Trust has earned an enviable reputation, and its tenets are well respected by all who go to the hills for quiet enjoyment. On Ladhar Bheinn the trust is trying primarily to regenerate the native Caledonian pine woods. We wandered along the stalkers' path that traces its way through the remnants of the upper woods before crossing the fast-flowing waters of the Allt Coire Dhorrcail.

We were in search of ancient shielings.

David Craig the historian, the collector of the oral tradition, the enquirer into ancient ways, was in full flow. 'People generally have it wrong about shielings,' he told me. 'Most think the ruins of the cottages are shielings, some sort of generic term, but the shielings were special. These were the places the women and children would come to in the summer months with the cattle, away from the muddy lanes and mess of the townships, up into the clear and vibrant air of the upper glens and corries. And there were no ministers to keep an eye on them either!'

He had noticed some markings on the new OS map of Knoydart, published in 1994, which showed some shielings in Coire Dhorrcail. He suspected that the OS may have got it wrong, but it hadn't.

After searching for twenty minutes or so, we found the tell-tale sign – a bright green patch on the hillside, the richness of the grass a sure sign of regular animal manuring. Just above it we found the circular stone foundation of the old shieling. Branches and turf would have been carried up here and built, tepee-like, on top of the ring of stone. These were temporary homes, for the summer only, where the women and children would live while the cattle enjoyed the fresher pastures of the higher glens and corries.

It was some time before I could drag David away from his search for other rings, but by now the rain had stopped, the sun had pierced the gloomy sky, and the clouds were tearing themselves apart to reveal blue skies and the magnificence of Coire Dhorrcail.

A horseshoe of ridges and peaks encloses the corrie to form this high cirque of riven cliffs and buttresses still rimmed by sparkling snow cornices. Our route was by the long, bumpy ridge of the Druim a' Choire Odhair which rises gently in stages, each protuberance offering grander and wider views out over Loch Hourn towards Beinn Sgritheall and Skye.

The summit, at 3346 feet (1020 m), is close to where this long ridge abuts on to the main ridge. The cairn itself is on the west-north-west ridge just a few yards from the junction, and as we approached it from Coire Dhorrcail we gasped in wonder. To our right, cloud and mist rolled upwards out of the neighbouring Choire Odhair, while everything to the left of the summit ridge, as far as the eye could see, was clear and in sunshine. To add to the contrast, the demarcation line between the sun and the mist was formed by the vivid white line of the cornice, so intense that we had to screw our eyes up tight against the brightness of it.

Ladhar Bheinn is not only a magnificent mountain but a complex one, rising above a series of corries that bite into its steep north-eastern slopes. Our descent to the Màm

ABOVE: OUR ROUTE TO THE SUMMIT OF LADHAR BHEINN WAS BY WAY OF THE LONG AND BUMPY DRUIM A'
CHOIRE ODHAIR WHICH RISES IN FAIRLY GENTLE STAGES FROM THE SHORES OF LOCH HOURN.

RIGHT: CAMERON MCNEISH AND RICHARD ELSE IN COIRE DHORRCAIL OF LADHAR BHEINN. THIS SIDE
OF THE MOUNTAIN IS OWNED BY THE JOHN MUIR TRUST, A CONSERVATION BODY NAMED AFTER THE
SCOTS-BORN ENVIRONMENTALIST WHO BECAME THE FATHER FIGURE OF
AMERICAN NATIONAL PARKS.

•

Barrisdale followed the line of these corries, down to the Bealach Coire Dhorrcail, around the head of another steep corrie before the junction with the long Aonach Sgoilte ridge, and then down to another bealach before Stob a' Chearcaill and the long, wet slippery slopes which lead down eastwards to the Màm Barrisdale and our second camp.

Màm Barrisdale to Inverie

•

From the summit of Màm Barrisdale, easy slopes lead eastwards to Bachd Mhic an Tosaich, from where the ridge to Luinne Bheinn both narrows and steepens in a rough and rocky climb to the summit ridge. It's interesting that the name has been translated as meaning 'hill of anger', or 'hill of melody' or even 'hill of mirth' – a fair range of emotions. One Gaelic-speaking friend suggested it perhaps should just be 'hill of moods'!

The summit sits proudly at 3081 feet (939 m), offering fine views down the length of Gleann an Dubh-Lochain and out to Loch Nevis. Beyond, shimmering on a flat sea, were the dim outlines of Rhum and Eigg.

At the eastern end of the summit ridge, a steep southern flank drops down to a broad knolly ridge which eventually forms Druim Leac a' Shith. This ridge borders the remote and desolate northern corrie of Meall Buidhe, Knoydart's other Munro, and eventually leads you to the obviously defined north-east summit ridge. The highest of the two tops is the westernmost one, at 3104 feet (946 m).

A long ridge, high above Gleann Meadail, eventually brings you down from the high tops and into the lower reaches of Gleann an Dubh-Lochain, where a good Land Rover track swiftly carries you down into Inverie. But before we took that track to Inverie and the promise of a pint or two in the Forge Inn, we wanted to look at the first of two Knoydart memorials. Both represent different factions in an argument closely linked with the ongoing problem of Highland clearances.

On a knoll high above the Land Rover track is a beehive-shaped memorial to the family of Lord Brocket, a brooding presence which even today stands in defiance of all that is good and just. I cannot, for the life of me, understand why this monument has never been pulled down, stone by stone, the memory obliterated for ever. Let me tell you why I feel like this.

It's the story of an incident which took place in 1948, the story of seven local men, angered at the changes forced by an uncaring landlord on the place where they lived. Rather than simply accept what was happening to their homes, they decided to fight for justice. They believed passionately that they had a moral right to form crofts and to work the land that was deliberately being allowed to go to waste, asserting that they were the subject of twentieth-century land clearance – this time to make way for deer and rich sportsmen instead of sheep.

Their opponent, the uncaring landowner in question, was a millionaire brewer by the name of Arthur Ronald Nall-Cain, later to become Lord Brocket. An old Etonian and a graduate of Oxford, he spent some years as a barrister in London before becoming a Conservative MP, but his politics weren't confined purely to Britain. A stalwart member of the Anglo-German fellowship, he was friendly with Hitler and Ribbentrop and was well known as a Nazi sympathizer.

Brocket wanted to keep Knoydart for himself, his family and his sporting friends. He discouraged visitors. He made many of the older local employees redundant, and he refused to keep up the maintenance of the estate. Most of the locals had been working, in some shape or form, for the estate, but as soon as this source of employment was cut off people had to leave Knoydart to seek work elsewhere. The depopulation began all over again.

Eventually seven of the local men, not long returned from the war, realized that the only way they could live in peace and security was to take crofting land for themselves. Resorting to the tactics pioneered in the days of the Highland Land League, they staged a land raid, clearing small areas of land, marking them out, and claiming them as their own.

Their case was doomed from the start. Brocket had powerful friends and even the Labour government of the time singularly failed to help the men. After a lengthy legal battle, the men had to give up the land they had seized. Their brave effort is commemorated by another memorial, a small plaque set in a stone cairn in Inverie, its simplicity contrasting with the ostentatious, self-gratifying heap which stands high on its hill in Gleann an Dubh-Lochain.

JUSTICE!

•

In 1948, near this cairn, the Seven Men of Knoydart staked claims to secure a place to live and work.
For over a century Highlanders had been forced to use land raids to gain a foothold where
their forebears lived.
Their struggle should inspire each new generation of Scots to gain such rights by just laws.
History will judge harshly the oppressive laws that have led to the virtual extinction
of a unique culture from this beautiful place.

The sole survivor of those Seven Men of Knoydart, Archie MacDougall, now lives in Inverness. In his small book, *Knoydart – The Last Scottish Land Raid*, he suggests that the depopulation of the Highlands will continue until there is legislation to have a compulsory land register and to stop the purchase of undeveloped areas of land by speculators.

Despite the sorrow and injustice of this story, David and I completed our walk with a sense of hope. The locals we met in the Forge Inn were positive and looked forward to a future of better things. One keeper spoke highly of his employer, who loved Knoydart and was pouring money into his particular estate, while others told us of the families who were now living on the peninsula and of the deep sense of community there now was.

One such family is the Robinsons of Doune Marine. Alan and Mary Robinson, with their sons Jamie and Toby, came to Knoydart in the mid-1980s and set up a small business on the remote west coast. They now have several small chalets, a bunkhouse and a growing reputation for a place to which you can escape and enjoy the natural beauty of this wonderful area. Access to Doune is by boat, and the place is used by divers, sailors, ornithologists and walkers. Both Alan and Toby are excellent folk-singers, and a ceilidh had been arranged with musicians and singers coming from all over the peninsula for what turned out to be a great night of laughing, drinking, eating and singing.

As I battered out some sort of rhythm on an Irish bodhran (goatskin drum), with fiddles and guitars and voices in fine fettle, I realized that despite the Josephine Macdonnells and the Lord Brockets of this world there is still hope in Knoydart. The sense of community there is stronger than it has been for years, that spirit which can overcome the problems of access, remoteness and absentee landlords.

CHAPTER TWO

THE BLACKMOUNT

MINIMALISM MADE PURE

•

Cameron McNeish

A two-day mountain journey in the Blackmount Deer Forest

MAP: *OS 1:50 000 Sheet 50*

START AND FINISH: *Druimachoish, Glen Etive. Grid Ref: 136468*

LENGTH: *Approximately 17–18 miles (27–29 km)*

APPROXIMATE TIME: *2 days*

TERRAIN: *Uncompromising mountain walking*

ACCOMMODATION: *No accommodation in Glen Etive, but b&b, guest-houses and hotels in Bridge of Orchy and Glencoe. Private bunkhouses at Bridge of Orchy, Kingshouse and Glencoe, and a youth hostel in Glencoe. For good pub grub and an excellent range of real ale, try the Clachaig Inn in Glencoe, Scotland's premier climbers' inn usually offering good crack (friendly chat) and occasionally good folk music*

As one drives across Rannoch Moor from Bridge of Orchy to Glen Coe, the eye is captivated by a rising swell of steep-sided mountains that border the western fringe of the vast moor. They rise steeply above lonely Coire Ba, the largest natural amphitheatre in Scotland, the flatness of the foreground accentuating the long ridges and height of the hills.

These are the hills of the Blackmount Deer Forest, a compact group of mountains which is bounded by the upper reaches of Loch Etive in the west, by Glen Kinglass in the south, and by Rannoch Moor in the east. Although the Blackmount has few trees left, the area is a veritable forest of mountains. The eastern ramparts provide one of the finest high-level promenades in Scotland, the walk from between the two former cattle-drovers' inns at Inveroran and Kingshouse, across Stob Ghabhar, Clach Leathad (Clachlet) and Meall a' Bhuiridh. Only once does the ridge drop below 2500 feet (762 m), at the Bealach Fuar Chataidh, and the constant high elevation ensures the walker of some stunning views.

The view to the east is of course dominated by the huge expanse of Rannoch Moor, a mattress of peat, water and grassy hummocks. Away across the moor the shapely cone

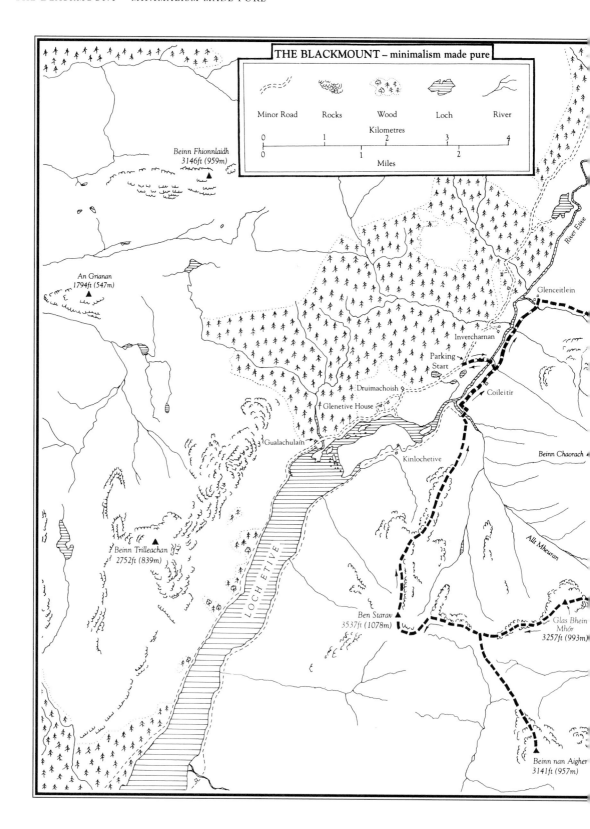

THE BLACKMOUNT – minimalism made pure

Minor Road　　Rocks　　Wood　　Loch　　River

Kilometres
0　　　　1　　　　2　　　　3　　　　4

Miles
0　　　　1　　　　2

Beinn Fhionnlaidh
3146ft (959m)

An Grianan
1794ft (547m)

River Etive

Glenceitlein

Invercharnan

Parking
Start

Druimachoish

Glenetive House

Coileitir

Gualachulain

Kinlochetive

Beinn Chaorach

LOCH ETIVE

Beinn Trilleachan
2752ft (839m)

Allt Mheuran

Ben Starav
3537ft (1078m)

Glas Bhein
Mhór
3257ft (993m)

Beinn nan Aigher
3141ft (957m)

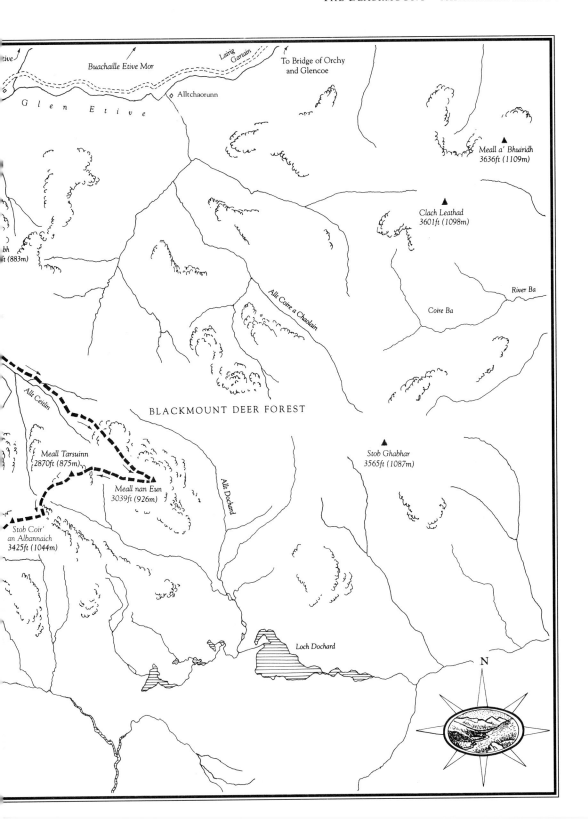

Laing
Gartain

To Bridge of Orchy
and Glencoe

Buachaille Etive Mor

Alltchaorunn

G l e n   E t i v e

Meall a' Bhuiridh
3636ft (1109m)

Clach Leathad
3601ft (1098m)

bh
t (883m)

Allt Coire a Chaolain

River Ba

Coire Ba

Allt Ceitlin

BLACKMOUNT DEER FOREST

Stob Ghabhar
3565ft (1087m)

Meall Tarsuinn
2870ft (875m)

Allt Dochard

Meall nan Eun
3039ft (926m)

Stob Coir'
an Albannaich
3425ft (1044m)

Loch Dochard

N

ABOVE: LOOKING ACROSS THE BARE DESOLATION OF RANNOCH MOOR TOWARDS THE EASTERN
FRINGES OF BLACKMOUNT DEER FOREST. THE HILLS RISE STEEPLY ABOVE LONELY COIRE BA, THE LARGEST
NATURAL AMPHITHEATRE IN SCOTLAND, THE FLATNESS OF THE FOREGROUND EMPHASIZING THE GRANDEUR
AND WILDNESS OF THE MOUNTAINS.

FAR LEFT: THE TWIN SUMMITS OF BUACHAILLE ETIVE BEAG AND BUACHAILLE ETIVE MOR
FROM GLEN ETIVE.

LEFT: THE BLACKMOUNT DEER FOREST IS NOT A FOREST AS SUCH, BUT HOME TO THOUSANDS OF RED DEER
WHICH IN WINTER CAN BE SEEN FORAGING ON THE LOWER SLOPES OF THE HILLS.

•

of Schiehallion stands sentinel, and to the north the protracted humps of the Glencoe hills lie in a complicated jumble, with Ben Nevis just lifting its whaleback above its neighbours. But perhaps the finest views, as they so often are, are to the west. So many people regard the Clachlet ridge as the only worthwhile ploy in these hills, but it isn't until you gaze across the panorama of peaks that you realize the interior of the forest is equally as fine.

A medley of higher and lower peaks all compete for the eye, all interlaced by high and tight ridges, many of them almost as lofty as the hills they connect. This is a high and lonely place, the hills composed mainly of granite, the southern and western slopes grassy, and the northern and eastern sides craggy, steep and dramatic: an area where the solitude-seeking walker can lose himself for a few days, collecting, if he wants, up to nine Munros.

In several crossings of Clachlet, on foot and on ski, I had always gazed longingly westwards to these other Blackmount hills before the opportunity arose to spend a couple of days exploring them at will.

It was eventually, unashamedly, a lightweight Munro-bagging raid: to use a couple of Americanisms, power-hiking as opposed to slackpacking! A power-hiker generally seeks a test rather than a therapy; the important thing is to walk far and effectively and, as often is the case when climbing Munros, to climb as many as possible within your given time-constraint. Slackpacking is a slower, more relaxed and leisurely pursuit where the important factor is simply to be there, soaking up the resonances and atmosphere of the green world. While the power-hiker will carry a minimalist kit, certainly less than 20 pounds (9 kg) for two or three days, the slackpacker will want more of the comforts that go with his or her more leisurely pace.

Now I should point out here that my normal backpacking practice, particularly as I get older, leans sharply in the direction of the slackpacker. Most of my trips nowadays take the form of therapy, a healing process designed to ease the tensions, the stresses and the problems that inevitably build up in an average week of twentieth-century living. The last thing I want to do on such jaunts is to burden myself with more time-tables, schedules and pressure to achieve. But having said that, sometimes, just some-times, I sense a need to hone up the muscles and the cardio-vascular system, to sharpen my physical fitness or, inevitably, simply to assure myself that I can still do it. 'I loved the garish day, and, in spite of fears, Pride ruled my will: remember not past years,' wrote Cardinal Newman. All that I usually prove to myself is that I'm not as fit as I would like to be, and so the next several trips tend to be in the power-hiking category simply to try to improve my fitness. No doubt I'll grow out of it eventually.

The five western Munros that lie nearer the Loch Etive side of the group offer a nice little round of about seventeen miles – more than possible in a big hill day, but the attraction of a high-level camp is always appealing. Access to these hills means a long drive down Glen Etive – no great hardship in itself, as the road winds and twists down the glen below the frowning crags of the Buachaille Etive Mor. This upper part of the glen is dominated by the twin guardians of Etive, Stob na Broige, the southern top of the Buachaille Etive Mor massif, and Stob Dubh of Buachaille Etive Beag. The pass of the Lairig Gartain rises steeply between the two to form a classic 'saddle'. All this is the storied land of Deirdre of the Sorrows, who, in the first century, fled from her native Ulster in the company of the Three Sons of Uisnach, to escape the jealous wrath of Concubar MacNessa, the High King. Here she roamed with her lover Naoise, fishing the foaming waters of the Etive, scaling the steep slopes of Ben Starav and Beinn Trilleachan, until a messenger sent from Ireland persuaded Naoise to return to his own land. MacNessa, seemingly, had forgiven Deirdre and the Three Sons and bade them come home. He promised to return the three brothers to their rightful roles as Knights of the Red Branch, the hereditary Order of Knighthood from which the kings of Ulster were chosen.

Deirdre, however, with typical female discernment, was deeply suspicious of the king's motives, and pleaded with Naoise to stay in Scotland. Her protestations in vain, she went with the three brothers back to Emhain Macha, the seat of the High King of Ulster. On seeing Deirdre again, MacNessa fell into a deep wrath born of jealousy and had Naoise and his brothers slain in an attempt to win the beautiful Deirdre for himself. Horrified, Deirdre fell into a deep depression and killed herself, never to see the shores of Etive again.

Glen Etive to the bealach between Ben Starav and Glas Bheinn Mhór

•

To one who spends a lot of time in the land-locked Cairngorms, the combined smell of bog myrtle and sea tang is a heady tonic, and with this mixture filling my senses I left the car at Druimachoish, close to where the river meets the loch, and retraced my steps along the road until I could cross the footbridge at Coileitir.

As the two Buachailles dominate the view to the north, so does Ben Starav dwarf the southwards one. The western slopes of this hill tumble down over 3000 feet to sea-level at Loch Etive's shore, and the fine peak is the culmination point of no fewer than five ridges, particularly beautiful in winter when snow forms sweeping cornices. I decided to leave Ben Starav until the end, when, hopefully, a sunset would grace the far-flung views westwards out towards Mull and beyond.

It was good to have a lightweight pack – about 15 pounds (7 kg), an indulgence in weightlessness. While I wouldn't describe myself necessarily as a backpacking

ABOVE: GLEN ETIVE AND THE BLACKMOUNT MAKE UP THE STORIED LAND OF DEIRDRE OF
THE SORROWS, WHO, IN THE FIRST CENTURY, CAME TO SCOTLAND FROM ULSTER TO ESCAPE THE UNWANTED
ATTENTIONS OF CONCUBAR MACNESSA, THE HIGH KING.

FAR LEFT: LEAVING MEALL NAN EUN BEFORE TACKLING THE AWKWARD ASCENT OF STOB COIR' AN
ALBANNAICH, THE HILL OF THE SCOTSMAN'S CORRIE.

LEFT: TEMPERATURE INVERSION TURNS THE BLACKMOUNT SUMMITS INTO ISLANDS ON A VAST
SEASCAPE OF CLOUD.

•

minimalist, after almost thirty years of pounding trails and hiking hills I'm more than convinced that 'light is right'. The lighter the weight of your pack, the further you can walk and the higher you can climb – and do so without suffering any of the beast-of-burden symptoms that are normally associated with carrying a heavy pack.

Working on the presumption that any fool can be uncomfortable, there are obviously basic and essential items of kit that must go into the pack – shelter, food and a means of cooking it – but over and above these essentials come the personal favourites – the gadgets. The tiny candle lantern which casts its yellow glow through the dark hours of evening, the hip-flask of whisky which casts its warm glow through the body, the paperback book (in the normal course of my life I find little time for reading, whereas on holidays and backpacking trips books are devoured eagerly).

Just as my preferred discipline is normally more in the slackpacking mould, so my pack usually equates with that more luxurious, easy-going methodology. But two or three times a year I've found it good practice to carry less, in fact as little as I can. But there are conditions for such trips. First of all I need a good weather forecast. Although the basic kit will protect me from normal summer conditions I'm too grey in the beard to risk a real miserable bout of weather. And because the camping aspect of backpacking is so enjoyable, I tend to use the ultra-light kit only when I want to move relatively quickly – those occasions when 'pride rules my will'. This was a good opportunity – two good hill days broken down conveniently into nine miles and eight miles.

Meall nan Eun is a 3039-feet (926-m) Munro which lies behind the headwaters of the Allt Ceitlin, a feeder of the River Etive. The higher you climb up this glen, the finer grows the view behind you. The dense greenery of the forests on the western slopes of Glen Etive soon give way to high peaks, An Grianan and Beinn Fhionnlaidh, with the barely recognizable (from this angle) Glencoe peaks to the north-west.

Meall nan Eun hides its summit from the rocky glen floor and is probably best ascended by following the Allt Ceitlin to its source on the bealach between Meall Tarsuinn and Meall nan Eun itself. I left my pack here, as shortly I had to return the same way to reach the next summit, Stob Coir' an Albannaich, at 3425 feet (1044 m).

The summit of Meall nan Eun is merely the highest point on a broad flat ridge, an unexciting place which offered meek consolation with its views of the rest of the day's walk. Beyond the ridge of the next Munro, Stob Coir' an Albannaich, Glas Bheinn Mhór and Ben Starav appeared. As an outlier to the connecting ridges, Beinn nan Aighenan, my other Munro for the day, looked far out of the way.

Stob Coir' an Albannaich ('the hill of the corrie of the Scotsman') is a fine hill, the corrie of its name holding snow well into the summer. I climbed it by a prominent gully from the bealach which connects it to Meall Tarsuinn. The top is the culmination of a long ridge which drops down to flat ground near Loch Dochard in the south-east.

In the craggy corrie of Albannaich's north-west shoulder, Beinn Chaorach, stands a striking pinnacle, Patey's Old Man. The rock-climbing description in the *Scottish*

Mountaineering Club Guide leaves no one in any doubt as to the dubiousness of the rock: 'Lasso the top and climb the rope.' Almost as an afterthought it goes on to say: 'Treat gently.'

The same guidebook recommends careful mapreading if the next top in the round, Glas Bheinn Mhór, is to be negotiated in mist. I had perfect weather and first-class visibility, which was perhaps just as well as the guidebook description is of the type to birl a tired brain into easy submission: 'First south of west, then east of south, before turning south-west to gain the ridge.' In actual fact, if you are accurate, a bearing can be taken from the summit of Stob Coir' an Albannaich to the bealach between its south-west slopes and the ridge which ascends Glas Bheinn Mhór.

Glas Bheinn Mhór itself can be seen clearly from Glen Etive: a round dumpy hill with high eastern and western ridges. A subsidiary unnamed top separates it from Ben Starav.

To the south, Beinn nan Aighenan (3141 feet/957 m) looms large, perhaps the least visited Munro of the whole area. This is not too surprising; with Ben Starav so temptingly close as the first day draws to an end, it is all too easy to leave Aighenan for another day. So many Munro-baggers build up a good list of solitary, isolated summits, all left for another day, almost all of them necessitating a full day or more for the privilege of ticking off a single in the tables. Don't make Beinn nan Aighenan another!

For the purposes of this little excursion, I did leave Aighenan for the morrow – an easy walk out and back in the morning without the pack, which I would pick up on my return before tackling Ben Starav. The bealach made a good bivouac site, with running water not far down in the corrie. As I crawled into my bivvy bag – less than 2 pounds (1 kg) in weight – the dying sun's rays were hitting the hills of the south – Beinn a' Chochuill, Beinn Eunaich and Cruachan – in a pink and red flourish. I dropped off to the melancholy music of a golden plover.

The Starav bealach to Druimachoish

•

Leaving my pack on the Ben Starav bealach, I dropped down to the lowest point (2000 feet/610 m) since leaving Meall nan Eun before taking the rocky scramble of Aighenan's north-west ridge. It was well worth the effort. Cruachan Beinn laid out its tops in full view to the south, and the morning sun was already casting long shadows over the lower reaches of Loch Etive. The high hills of Mull stood out in full relief, and further south the well-defined Paps of Jura peeped over the mainland hills. To the east, Loch Dochard sparkled like silver, with the pine-clad shores of Loch Tulla stretching out to the hills fringing the south of Rannoch Moor, Beinn an Dòthaidh, Beinn Achaladair and Beinn a' Chreachain.

ABOVE: THE MOUNTAINS OF THE BLACKMOUNT DEER FOREST, A COMPACT GROUP OF HIGH HILLS
WHICH IS BOUNDED BY THE UPPER REACHES OF LOCH ETIVE IN THE WEST, GLEN KINGLASS IN THE SOUTH
AND RANNOCH MOOR IN THE EAST.

RIGHT: LOOKING INTO THE DARK DEPTHS OF GLEN ETIVE FROM THE SUMMIT SLOPES OF BEN STARAV.
THE BIDEAN NAM BIAN MASSIF OF GLEN COE IS PROMINENT ON THE LEFT.

•

I had left Ben Starav until last, and I was glad that I had. The narrow eastern ridge offers a good scramble on shattered quartzite-streaked granite, a classic little ridge with everything you could ask for, except, unfortunately, any real exposure. A flat and grassy plateau leads to the final summit and a trig point where, in early summer, moss campion makes eye-catching little patches against the steel grey of the screes. A ptarmigan made an awkward and croaky retreat as I approached, and there below, in its long stretched-out splendour, was Loch Etive.

To the north-east, mountains stood out in an endless jumble; the air was still and I could faintly hear the steady pulsing of some diesel-engined craft down on the loch, 3000 feet (914 m) below. The long and narrow north-east ridge wound gently down to the head of the loch and my awaiting vehicle, bringing to an end a magnificent round of five Munros and seventeen or so miles of memorable mountain walking. I had enjoyed the bonus of meeting no other person, a justification, if any is needed, for a long stravaig (wander) in these hills rather than on the over-subscribed routes of nearby Glencoe.

I left, making the resolution that I would return and walk all its Munros, camping high again on the intersecting ridges. Better still, I might just take a week and lose myself amid that jumble of blue-remembered hills, wandering with the ghosts of Deirdre and the Three Sons of Uisnach, soaking up the atmosphere and the memories. Of such things is heaven made.

CHAPTER THREE

MULL

A VISIT TO KENNY'S ISLAND

•

Richard Else

A three- to four-day walk through a variety of mountainous landscapes

---

MAPS: *OS 1:50 000 Sheets 48 and 49*

START AND FINISH: *By the ruin of Torness, on the A849. Grid Ref: 649327*

LENGTH: *30 miles (48 km)*

APPROXIMATE TIME: *3–4 days, depending on the exact route chosen*

TERRAIN: *Rough walking especially on the lower ground. A compass can be unreliable on Mull because of the magnetic nature of some rock, and the ridge between A' Chioch and Ben More may require care in adverse conditions*

ACCOMMODATION: *The Glenforsa Hotel in Salen is welcoming to walkers, has a good bar and will provide drying facilities. Tobermory has a number of good hotels, b&b, restaurants and cafés but, like the campsites, many are not open outside the tourist season. The Western Isles Hotel provides traditional Highland hospitality with excellent food, and a stay there is a well-deserved reward*

TRANSPORT: *The most useful ferry is from Oban to Craignure. Although buses coincide with the ferry's arrival, they are of limited value and a car or bike is a better option for exploring the island*

To a greater or lesser extent, every long walk brings with it a measure of uncertainty. Once you leave the car or bus you are on your own. You break free of the usual ties, and apart from perhaps a pre-arranged pick-up point you are free not only to make any choices you wish but, to look at it from the converse angle, you also have to respect any obstacles along the way and take note of them. It is this measure of uncertainty that I find one of the most attractive aspects of a journey into the wilderness. In some small part this experience should shape you and, just like a longer expedition, you should come back not only renewed and invigorated (if exhausted!) but you should also return changed. That is exactly what happened on one autumn trip to Mull.

First I have a confession to make. For many years I had neglected Mull: it was always passed on frantic journeys further north to mountains that, while higher, lack

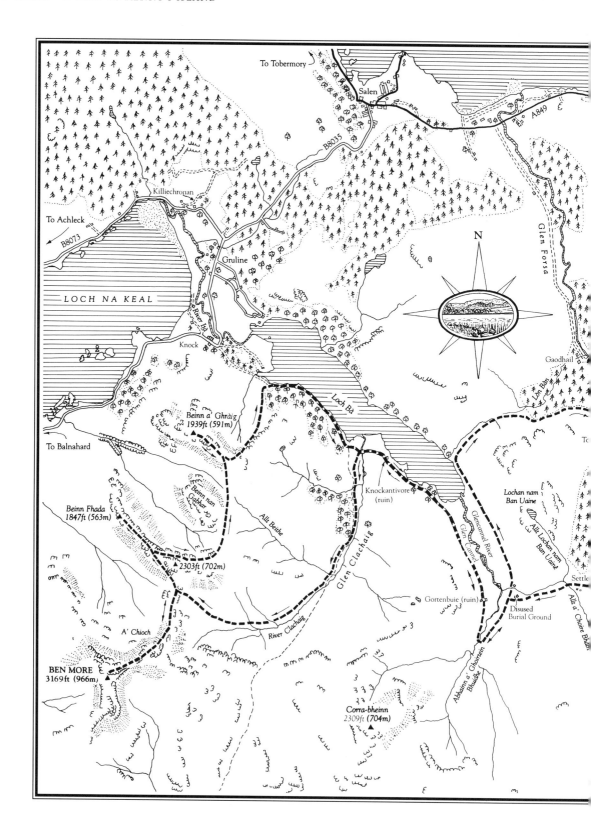

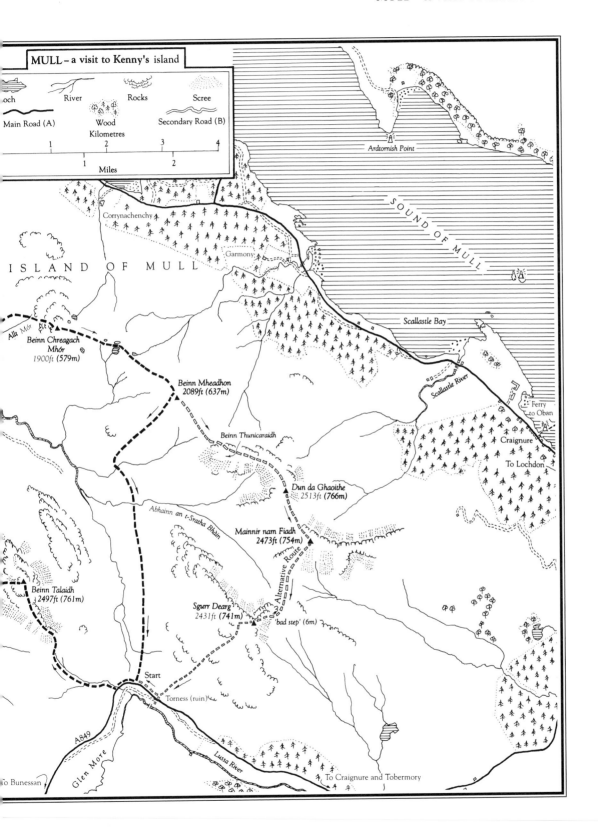

MULL – a visit to Kenny's island

Loch   River   Rocks   Scree

Main Road (A)   Wood   Secondary Road (B)
Kilometres
1   2   3   4
1   2
Miles

Ardtornish Point

SOUND OF MULL

Corrynachenchy

Garmony

ISLAND OF MULL

Scallastle Bay

Allt Mòr

Beinn Chreagach
Mhòr
1900ft (579m)

Beinn Mheadhon
2089ft (637m)

Scallastle River

Ferry
to Oban

Craignure

To Lochdon

Beinn Thunicaraidh

Dun da Ghaoithe
2513ft (766m)

Abhainn an t-Sratha Bhàin

Mainnir nam Fiadh
2473ft (754m)

Beinn Talaidh
2497ft (761m)

Sgurr Dearg
2431ft (741m)

Alternative Route

'bad step' (6m)

Start

Torness (ruin)

A849

Glen More

Lussa River

To Bunessan

To Craignure and Tobermory

in many ways the remoteness of those on Mull. It's that remoteness that also comes as a surprise. Unless you know the island very well indeed – and that can take a good many years – you simply do not think of it as a wilderness area. This impression is also confirmed by a cursory look at the map, which gives, I think, a misleading impression that there is no spot too far from either a habitation or a road. Yet the roads are tiny and often cling precariously to the landscape, the habitations are far smaller than their names would suggest, and the land can be wild and hard to travel through.

Kenny had suggested that I should take a closer look at the island. He is our commissioning editor at BBC Scotland and someone who is keen on the outdoors. An extremely keen sailor rather than a walker, he was born and bred on the island, coming from a family that has inhabited this landscape for many generations. In between chatting about how the boat he helped crew was going, the trials of inshore racing and insisting that he was 'just a weekend sailor', we had often spoken about the films I was making and what constitutes a wilderness area. 'Go to Mull,' Kenny had said, 'and I am not just saying that because I come from there. But go again and let me know what you think.'

On the short ferry crossing from Oban one day in late October, I had been listening to two fiddlers and an accordionist in the bar and idly turning over an idea in my mind. Should you, I thought, plan a long walk in every detail or be more reactive and follow your instincts and whims? Which would be more in tune with nature? In truth, I had spent days poring over the OS maps trying to finalize my plans. With public transport on the island less than ideal (especially out of season), I wanted a walk that would start and finish from the same place, but also one that would allow me sufficient flexibility to change my plans if necessary. Being a true Libran, and looking forward to spending my birthday during the walk, I had only just made a decision on arrival at Craignure. My real problem was this: I did not want my walk to be dominated by the island's only Munro, Ben More, but I did want to include it in my itinerary. I also wanted to look from as many angles as possible at the effects of the volcanic activity that has shaped so much of this landscape. Finally, I wanted to see some of the many changes, not all of which are for the better, taking place in the landscape.

Torness to Glen Cannel

•

Leaving MacBrayne's ferry and travelling south-west on the A849 it looked as if Mull had gone on holiday and, in view of what happened during the next few days, that might not have been a bad idea! I left my Land Rover on the sharp bend on the road near the ruin of Torness (reference 642328) with the thought of climbing up Beinn Talaidh (which translates as 'hill of the cattle or livestock'), before heading further west. This shapely mountain is 2497 feet (761 m) and you have nearly all of that ascent to undertake from the road. I was struck immediately by the recent afforestation at this end of Glen Forsa, which although shown only in outline on the 1:50 000 OS map, is more accurately portrayed on the larger-scale 1:25 000 one. Yet this is only a small scar on the side of a distinctive mountain, which is an elegantly shaped cone with a sense of grandeur emphasized by its relative isolation. After initially walking west to avoid the deer fence, I contoured north and approached the summit by its fine south-east ridge. It is a good, solid pull up, but after the rough lower slopes the ground is firm underfoot and I reached the top in good time, but not before the wind had risen and was battering my fleece. After many hot months followed by an Indian summer, this came as a shock to the system! I had come away in what looked like a period of settled high pressure, but the western horizon suggested that the weather might not be quite as settled as I expected. On the summit dome, which is a mixture of grass and stones, you'll find an OS triangulation pillar curiously set in a column (as opposed to the usual shape). Although the cloud-level was not much higher than the summit, I still had a good panorama with views away north to the top of Glen Forsa, the very eastern tip of Loch na Keal and the Sound of Mull, while to the west the top of Ben More, some 650 feet higher, stubbornly refused to reveal itself.

I had planned to descend off the western flank of Beinn Talaidh, and neither the steepness nor the roughness of the ground proved an obstacle – although I was glad to be using my walking-poles. Twelve months previously I had scorned the idea of walking-poles, but now I am totally converted to their use, especially when travelling on multi-day trips with a full pack. Just before I reached the Allt a' Choire Bhàin I was suddenly stopped by the remains of stone dwellings. I had noticed them marked on the 1:25 000 map but was not prepared for what I saw. Perhaps it was the time of day – it was late afternoon with long shafts of sunshine breaking through the overcast sky – or just my mood, but this settlement made an enormous impact on me. Of course, you can hardly wander anywhere on Scotland's west coast without being painfully aware of the Clearances and their aftermath, but somehow, at this particular moment and in this particular place, I was thinking not about a pile of stones but of fellow human beings and how they lived their lives. To think back less than 200 years and imagine a life that began in this glen on Mull and ended, perhaps, in the New World of Canada is hard to conceive. We might struggle intellectually to understand what happened to these people, but I am doubtful if we can fully comprehend emotionally. Once there had been a community here; now there was just the wind blowing through the rough grass, and the stones standing as a silent witness. Historians will argue that places like Mull were, in any case, over-grazed and that some form of 'clearance' would have been necessary, but that is, I think, to avoid the main issue. What is so appalling is the manner in which the Scottish Clearances were enforced and the catastrophic impact they had on the lives of so many working people.

ABOVE: BEN MORE, MULL'S ONLY MUNRO, PROVIDES SUPERB PANORAMIC VIEWS. THIS VISTA,
TO THE NORTH-WEST, PROVIDES AN OUTSTANDING VIEW OF LOCH NA KEAL, THE ISLAND OF EORSA AND
THE NORTH-WEST HILLS OF MULL.

LEFT: A' CHIOCH AND BEN MORE FROM GLEN MORE.

•

I now followed the western bank of the Allt a' Choire Bhàin, saw it join the Allt Lochan nam Ban Uaine to become Glencannel River, and followed the river, tumbling and cascading on its journey west. I passed the site of the burial ground, although the most notable features are a jumbled mass of stone walls, wooden fencing and a ruined building dating from more recent times. Perhaps I missed the obvious in my haste to move onwards, but I saw no evidence of headstones or similar artefacts.

Now, in the late afternoon, the golds, greens and browns were softening, and with a last look at Beinn Talaidh I made my way south up-river by the Abhainn a' Ghoirtein Bhuidhe and soon found an ideal campsite opposite and further upstream from the ruin of Gortenbuie. With the shorter days of autumn, darkness was falling quickly. I started to pitch my tent and noticed that the wind had gathered momentum and was starting to rush down the upper reaches of Glen Cannel. In the few minutes it took to erect the tent, that rush had turned into a roar, and a big storm was on its way in from the south-west. As I cooked my meal, I was pleased to have a reliable shelter but also conscious that even though the tent was pitched right into the wind it was already taking a beating – and all this at virtually sea-level. Usually I like to camp high, but I was pleased on this occasion to be in the glen.

As the hours of darkness went by, the tent was continually bombarded with rain and high winds, one sounding like rapid artillery fire, the other creating a continuous wall of sound. I had experienced similar ferocious storms on Lewis, but this one was one of the worst I had heard and more resembled the terrific storms you often get in the high mountains. I was impressed by how well the tent stood up to such a constant battering, and it was only at dawn that the wind abated to a more reasonable level. Only then did I hear a different type of noise. I awoke to find that the river, which is some twenty-odd feet across at this point, had risen a foot or more during the night and all but the smallest streams were now potentially dangerous to cross. I looked out of my tent to see many new silver ribbons of water making their way down the hillside and remembered how many people have drowned crossing Scottish rivers in spate. Making the first coffee of the day, I also remembered it was my birthday.

Glen Cannel to Beinn Fhada
via Ben More

•

At first I thought that any high-level walking would be impossible, but as the day got lighter I realized that by modifying my plans a good hill day would still be possible. Instead of heading immediately for higher ground, I eventually crossed the

Glencannel River further upstream and, having retraced my steps on the other side to the shore of Loch Bà I crossed the River Clachaig and walked up its north-western side. The rain still continued to beat down, driven by a wind that was rapidly resuming its previous ferocity. Looking up, I saw the sheets of rain pound down the glen in a rhythmic formation. Normally I would not choose to be out on a day like this (and I didn't see anyone else who was!), but the crossing of streams in full spate soon became a mental as well as a physical challenge and I often relied on the support of my walking-poles to make sure I managed to keep my footing. A number of detours were necessary, and even walking over the rough lower ground of the glen became a boggy ordeal. Every so often the deluge would lessen for a while, but the tops stubbornly refused to shed their wreaths of mist and then the storm would come right in again.

Stopping for a short lunch snack (after all, when you are that wet it does not matter much if you have a break), I noticed that the Allt Beithe, which I had crossed without too much difficulty, had now swollen so much that a return crossing would have been difficult. I also thought that some of our preconceptions about a wilderness area can, on occasions, be quite inaccurate. We often presume, for example, that such areas are peaceful and quiet. Sometimes that is true, but for the last twelve hours and more my ears had been assaulted by a cacophony of sound. The decibel-level seemed as loud as a rock concert! It had started with the wind (which was amplified enormously as it hit my tent) but now it was the sheer volume of water running down every available route on the hillside that was making the most noise. When wind and water joined together, the noise was positively deafening.

Ignoring the path that crosses the River Clachaig, which was just as well in the circumstances, I continued a slow but sure height gain until I arrived at the bealach separating Beinn Fhada from A' Chioch. Following the sharp but shapely ridge that eventually leads to the top of Ben More (a name that simply means 'big hill') took a certain amount of determination. After an initial hesitation I had got into a measured step and that certain sort of 'head down and keep going' mentality that has its own pleasure. I just kept following the ridge upwards until, after some scrambling, I finally reached the summit and the large circular shelter. On a fine day there are spectacular views from here, but now there was nothing but wind and rain. Nevertheless I felt a real sense of achievement and, unwilling to be robbed of any view, I dropped off the north-west flank until I was below the cloud base. The effort was worthwhile, for I was greeted with a majestic, sombre panorama that included the landforms of Eorsa and Ulva, while away to the western horizon the outline of the Treshnish Islands was etched clearly in the distance. Standing there, in the wind and the rain, and feeling exceedingly damp, I couldn't think of a better way of spending my birthday!

Some retracing of my steps was necessary, as I wanted to take in two other tops in this immediate vicinity. The first of these is Beinn Fhada (appropriately named 'the long hill') with its elongated summit ridge sweeping north-westwards from a high

Above: Looking east from the summit of Ben More, a name that means simply 'big hill', the shapely ridge leads east-north-east towards its smaller outlier, A' Chioch. The ascent of these two hills makes a splendid outing in its own right but can also be incorporated into a more ambitious day out that includes ascents of Beinn Fhada and Beinn a' Ghràig.

Right: Much of the interest of walking on Mull can be found in tiny details like the lichen clinging to ancient walls.

•

point of 2303 feet (702 m) to a subsidiary summit of 1847 feet (563 m) at the far end. As so often on Mull, the higher you get the better the walking becomes, and the walk along Beinn Fhada's ridge and back again was especially enjoyable. I did so with two, unconnected thoughts in my mind. First, I had clearly hit a spell of unsettled weather with a potential high-pressure area losing out to a succession of incoming lows. 'Competing weather systems' is the official jargon, I think, but that might be a little unkind to the Met Office because I imagine that trying accurately to predict the weather along any part of Scotland's west coast is one of their more demanding tasks. Secondly, I have spent all my adult life in both written and visual media, concentrating alternately on one and then the other. Recently I had been spending more time with my camera, and I wondered whether words or image best captured the sense of this magical island, its variety of landscape and its traumatic history, a place that, in common with many rural areas, faces a whole range of social and economic challenges. How, I thought, do you portray both a landscape and its people? Often I felt my camera would be the best tool, but I also wanted to capture an island whose population had not only shrunk from over 10 500 in 1821 to less than a quarter of that size but which was disproportionately short of people of working age and over-represented by those in retirement. You can, I thought, take only so many images of abandoned buildings and former settlements.

I suspect the majority of walkers ignore Beinn nan Gabhar on their way from Beinn Fhada to Beinn a' Ghràig. I followed this pattern, believing that in different surroundings it would be ascended more often. I kept to the higher parts of this plateau, avoiding the rougher ground, and found a good spot to stop. There is a real sense of space up here and it's a good place to settle into the wilderness.

Beinn a' Ghràig to Torness

•

Beinn a' Ghràig (meaning 'hill of the herd') is quite different in character from Beinn Fhada and, in my view, a hill not to be rushed. A short pull up to its southern extremity is accomplished easily, and you get two rewards for the effort: fine views down to Loch Bà, and the constantly changing rock formations on the top. I remember thinking I could spend many days up here just exploring and photographing these sculptured forms, which I had come to think of as one of Mull's characteristic features. Now, though, it was time to return eastwards, and I could see my next objective, Lòn Bàn, as a distinctive glen on the opposite side of Loch Bà. The descent to the loch is quick and attractive, and the walk by its shore and past the ruin of Knockantivore gave moody, brooding views down this long sheet of water.

Without much thought, other than how attractive Lòn Bàn was with the autumn colours renewed after the heavy rainfall, I set off down the glen. It was only some time later that I realized this was a mistake and that I would have been better making for the higher ground. What should have been an idyllic walk became extremely hard work, especially as the new rainfall made all progress slow and deliberate. In any event, this would have been hard walking over rough ground with tussocky grass alternating with half-hidden water-channels. Now it was a long hard slog and anyone watching might have been surprised to see me laughing at my own stupidity. With a full pack, my progress towards the northern end of Glen Forsa seemed to take for ever. To make matters worse, I even took the longer route around the southern part of the plantation instead of keeping to the northern side. All the time I had been following what looked a more attractive visual line instead of using my brain!

It was not much easier on the other side of the glen as I tramped up by the side of the Allt Mór to Beinn Chreagach Mhór (1900 feet/579 m). The ascent was long and exhausting but, apart from the forestry plantations (about which the less said the better), gave a superb view back to the west. For the first time I was beginning to feel a real sense of achievement. The weather was still unsettled and looked like remaining so, but the wind had died down and the rain was reduced to light showers. The Allt Mór was a delightful stream to accompany upwards, particularly the miniature ravines near the top. Away on the floor of Glen Forsa I could just see two other people who looked as if they had completed the long walk in from east of Salen. The summit of Beinn Chreagach Mhór (which translates as the 'big rocky ben') was every bit as rewarding as I had hoped, giving good views of this part of the island and across to the mainland. It also gave access to a superb ridge, and before I set off along it I spent a few minutes appreciating my present surroundings. They included views of the Sound of Mull and, away to the mainland, of Lochaline and the hills beyond.

Starting off towards Beinn Mheadhon I was impressed by the richness and diversity of this ridge, with its lochans and outcrops. From time to time I would walk over towards the eastern side to see how the landscape was revealing itself, while to the south was a splendid view of Sgurr Dearg with the 'bad step' on its eastern ridge silhouetted against the skyline. I wanted to walk the whole ridge, but the delays earlier in the walk meant that the shortened days of autumn were catching up with me and if I wanted to be down before nightfall some hard decisions would have to be made. Camping on the ridge itself would have been an attractive option, but I had arranged to meet my partner that night, so I reluctantly had to accept that time was running out. I wandered on engrossed in my own thoughts and saw, as I approached Beinn Mheadhon, that the view eastwards was constantly evolving.

Now, though, it was time for me to make my descent, and a long, rough route down meant that I contoured around the western slopes of Beinn Thunicaraidh and across the Abhainn an t-Sratha Bhàin before making my way alongside the forest and back to

MULL, LIKE ALL THE WESTERN ISLES, SUFFERS ITS FAIR SHARE OF BAD WEATHER,
BUT AT OTHER TIMES IT'S EASY TO UNDERSTAND THE PULL OF THE WEST WITH SUNSETS AS DRAMATIC
AS THOSE FOUND ANYWHERE.

•

the road. I do not think there is any particularly easy way here of avoiding the rough walking and, if time allows, keeping to the ridge and taking in Dun da Ghaoithe, Mainnir nam Fiadh and Sgurr Dearg is a better option. The descent from the latter is not only easy but offers excellent views southwards, reinforcing the old adage that Mull is full of variety and never dull.

Later, I wandered into the bar at the Glenforsa Hotel in Salen to find a number of regulars having their heads shaved in an event that seemed only partly to do with a local charity. As the evening progressed, the price went steadily upwards. As I settled into another pint, I also realized that Kenny had been right to draw my attention to a landscape that has been shaped equally by geological and human factors and is as fine a wilderness area as any in Scotland. That many of its hills are climbed relatively infrequently is an added bonus, here is a space in which you can make your plans but one in which you also have to respect the prevailing conditions. Which is exactly how it should be.

CHAPTER FOUR

THE MINIGAIG

TALES AND SUPERSTITION

•

Cameron McNeish

A two-day walk from Blair Atholl to Kingussie

MAPS: *OS 1:50:000 Sheets 42, 43 and 35*
START: *Blair Atholl. Grid Ref: 866663*
FINISH: *Kingussie. Grid Ref: 755005*
LENGTH: *30 miles (48 km)*
APPROXIMATE TIME: *2 days*
TERRAIN: *Footpaths, tracks and a section of wild exposed country over 2000 feet (610 m)*
ACCOMMODATION: *Blair Atholl is on the London–Inverness railway line and has a good range of b&bs, guest-houses and hotels. A very interesting working mill in the village sells good coffee and home baking: well worth a visit. Kingussie also has a good range of accommodation of all standards, plus a fish and chip shop. The Scot House Hotel offers an excellent range of bar meals. There is a private bunkhouse in Newtonmore, three miles away*

People tend to be one of two types: those who believe in ghosts and those who don't. I've always considered myself in the latter category, despite sometimes being faced with almost overwhelming evidence to the contrary. The hills of Scotland have a long tradition of the supernatural, which is hardly surprising since the indigenous Highlander, even today, leans towards the superstitious, and the history of Gaeldom is considerably more than splattered with tales of the second sight, the Little People, and tales from beyond the grave.

Neither is it unusual to hear such tales recounted by otherwise pragmatic mountaineers. Donald Watt, the one-time leader of the Lochaber Mountain Rescue Team, tells the tale of coming down from a hill on a very hot day and seeing a small cottage below him with smoke coming from the chimney. Someone was standing at the door. Deciding that he would stop and ask for a drink of water, he continued his descent behind a copse of wood which momentarily hid the cottage from view. When he reached the road in the glen and walked past the wood, he was astonished to find an

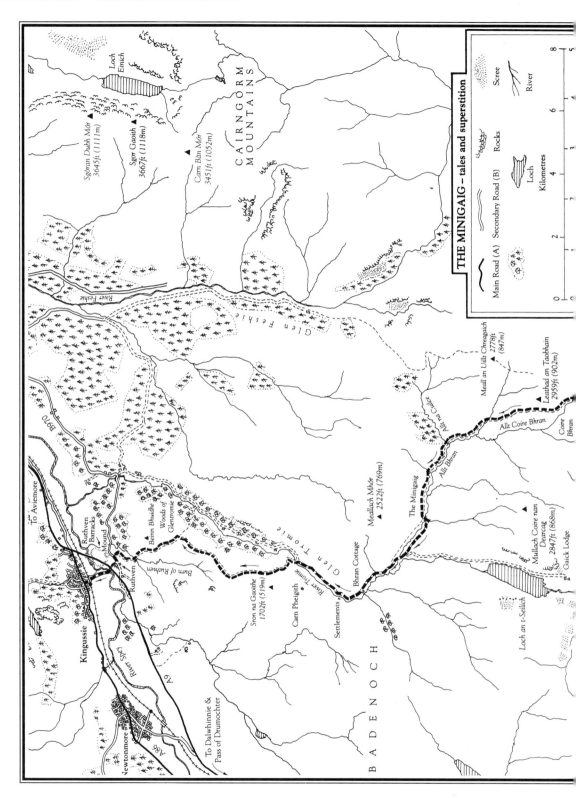

THE MINIGAIG – tales and superstition

Main Road (A)   Secondary Road (B)   Rocks

Scree

River

Loch

Kilometres

CAIRNGORM
MOUNTAINS

Loch
Einich

Sgòran Dubh Mòr
3645ft (1111m)

Sgor Gaoith
3667ft (1118m)

Carn Bàn Mòr
3451ft (1052m)

River Feshie

Glen Feshie

Allt na Caoire

Meall an Uillt Chreagaich
2778ft (847m)

Leathad an Taobhain
2959ft (902m)

Allt Coire Bhran

Coire
Bhran

B970

Allt Bhran

The Minigaig

Meallach Mhòr
2522ft (769m)

Benn Bhuidhe

Woods of
Glentromie

Mullach Coire nan
Dearcag
2847ft (868m)

Gaick Lodge

To Aviemore

Ruthven
Barracks

Mound

Ruthven

Burn of Ruthven

Sron na Gaoithe
1702ft (519m)

Carn Pheigith

River Tromie

Glen Tromie

Bhran Cottage

Settlements

Loch an t-Seilich

Kingussie

River Spey

A9

To Dalwhinnie &
Pass of Drumochter

A86

Newtonmore

BADENOCH

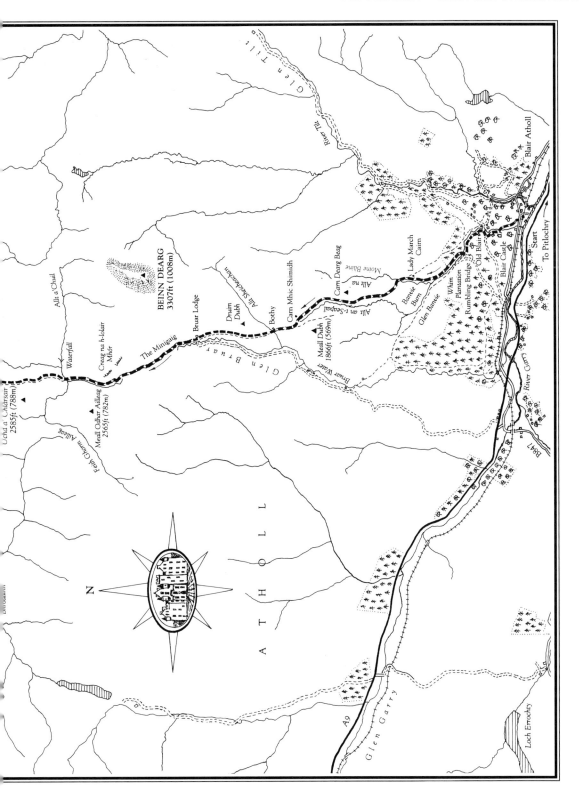

BEINN DEARG
3307ft (1008m)

Glen Tilt

River Till

Blair Atholl

Alla a'Chull

Allt Sheicheachan

Drum
Dubh

Bruar Lodge

Carn Mhic Shimidh

Carn Dearg Beag

Moine Bàine

Lady March
Cairn

Old Blair

Blair Castle

Start

To Pitlochry

The Minigaig

Creag na h-Iolair
Mhór

Bothy

Glen Bruar

Banvie
Burn

Glen Banvie

Whim
Plantation

Rumbling Bridge

Waterfall

Allt na

Allt an t-Seapail

Meall Dubh
1866ft (569m)

Bruar Water

River Garry

Ucha a'Chàrsair
2585ft (788m)

Meall Odhar Ailleag
2565ft (782m)

Fèith Chiaoin Ailleag

B847

N

A T H O L L

A9

Glen Garry

Loch Errochty

old ruin, a cluster of stones and a gable wall, where a few moments earlier he had seen a lived-in home. Creepy!

Another account, told by the mountaineer and writer Frank Smythe, is rather more lurid in detail. He was enjoying a walk in Kintail when he stopped to enjoy his lunch at the head of a small fold in the hills. As he sat and gazed down into this tiny pass, suddenly he was aware of people marching through it towards him, but they were people of another age – with plaids and bonnets and moccasins on their feet – they were pushing carts on which were piled great loads, possibly all their belongings. There were men and women and even some skulking dogs. As he gazed in amazement, he saw others run over the top of the hill towards the first group. They were carrying swords and targes and in seconds a horrible massacre took place. Smythe saw it all, and was helpless with fear. But as suddenly as it started it stopped – the dead and the dying were gone, and the small fold in the hills was as it had been earlier, a quiet and peaceful west Highland glen.

A number of years ago I walked over Comyns Road, a fourteenth-century hill track which runs over the marvellously remote eastern Grampians from Blair Atholl to Kingussie. At one point the 27-mile (43-km) route runs through a district known as Gaick, an area which, according to that wonderful old Scots sennachie (storyteller) Seton Gordon, is the most supernatural place in Scotland.

In his book, *Highways and Byeways in the Central Highlands*, Gordon tells the stories of Gaick – of the Leannan Sith, the fairy sweetheart who had the habit of appearing before hunters in the forest and entrancing them by her beauty, and of the tiny women dressed in green, doll-like creatures who, in the lonely confines of the higher corries, follow the herds of deer and milk the hinds like cattle. He also tells the tale of Col. Jimmy Dennis who, as recently as 1958 when deerstalking, looked through his glass and saw a small figure by the side of a stream. The figure was tiny, and wore a green cloak with a siren hood, like a tiny pixie. He took his glass from his eye, rubbed it, and looked again. The figure was gone. Later, as he related the tale to one of the local keepers, the old man looked at him, screwed up his eyes and said in a quiet voice: 'Then ye've seen the Sprite o' Gaick.'

The Highlands abound in such tales, and even in these mercifully emancipated decades many folk still tend to become alarmed at the thought of spending the night away from what we would regard as outposts of civilization – proper campsites with running water and preferably a clean toilet block, guest-houses or, at a pinch, youth hostels. When pushed for a logical explanation they rattle on about the cold, the discomfort, the necessity for the right equipment and experience. I've even heard those who express fear of being mugged. But the real barrier, I am convinced, is much less obvious. It's a basic fear of the unknown.

This phenomenon is of course exacerbated when you walk alone, and that's how I wanted to walk the Minigaig.

Like Comyns Road, the Minigaig runs from Blair Atholl to Kingussie in Badenoch, and replaced the older road some time before the seventeenth century. Comyns Road probably fell into disuse because the Minigaig was more direct and slightly shorter and, certainly, seventeenth-century maps show the Minigaig as the sole route across the Grampians.

John Kerr, a local Atholl expert in such matters, suggests that the Minigaig may not have come into existence until the completion of the old Tilt Bridge in Old Blair in the sixteenth century, as this would have provided a preferable crossing of the river for the drovers and their cattle *en route* to the trysts of the south.

Until General Wade built his new road over Drumochter Pass between Atholl and Badenoch, the main route through the wild and remote Grampians was by way of this high-level bridleway. The route lies across a great wedge of high, broken countryside which lies between the Pass of Drumochter in the west and the line of Glen Tilt, Glen Geldie and Glen Feshie in the east.

As I shouldered my pack at the great wrought-iron gates of Blair Castle, the words of a modern guidebook lay sullenly in my mind: 'The Minigaig... is perhaps the bleakest and most featureless terrain crossed by any major hill track. The track bypasses the very highest points on the moor to seek shelter from the elements, giving some sections of the route a peculiarly closed-in aspect that adds to one's feelings of being a mere speck of humanity in the vast, uncaring wilderness.'

Later on the guidebook cheerily reminds us that many have died on the Minigaig's open slopes. My concern wasn't so much for being a mere speck of humanity – some things we can't avoid – but the timing of my walk did concern me a bit. The Minigaig climbs to a height of about 2745 feet (837 m) between the headwaters of the Bruar and the Tromie, a stark, remote place of high, undulating moorland and wide open skies, deer infested and haunted by ptarmigan and eagle, not to mention the Leannan Sith and the spectral neighbours of the neighbouring Gaick hills... but I don't believe in such things. Do I?

No, I simply didn't want to camp out on top of this 'vast, uncaring wilderness' in December, with the possibility of wet, stormy weather blasting out of the west. December days may be short, but they can be fine, with the low sun picking out features on the hillsides and creating the long shadows normally associated with morning and evening. The problem is that such weather doesn't last long at this time of the year, and there's usually a system of low pressure lurking on the edge of the Atlantic waiting to pounce. And this more or less amounted to the forecast I had picked up that morning. I had to cross the high pass before the storm broke.

The short days of December added to my problem. At these northern latitudes it starts to become dark not long after 4 p.m. By 5 p.m. it is pitch black. Not only did I want to avoid being caught out by a storm on the Minigaig's high plateau, but I also wanted to get over its high point before I lost the precious hours of daylight.

Above: The Minigaig, just like Comyns Road, finishes at Ruthven Barracks just outside Kingussie. This military stronghold was last destroyed by followers of Charles Edward Stuart as they fled from the Battle of Culloden in 1746.

Right: Blair Castle, the start of the walk. The Duke of Atholl, who died recently, passed on the castle and the Atholl Estate to a charitable trust just before he died.

•

Blair Atholl to Coire Bhran

•

Blair Castle is whitewashed, as though to add a bit of brightness to the grey, douce village of Blair Atholl, and is home of the Duke of Atholl. The policies reflect much of modern tourism: drive 'em up in a coach, drag 'em past a few interpretive signs, and send 'em on their way again after a visit to the craft shop. I suppose this is merely another phase in the chequered history of Blair Castle, a history that goes back to the twelfth century, when John Comyn of Badenoch built his Cummings Tower.

Various alterations and adaptations have been made ever since, and the building is no stranger to royalty. In 1336 Edward III paid a social call, followed by Mary Queen of Scots in 1564, and the Marquis of Montrose garrisoned his army at the castle in 1644. A less sociable call was made by Oliver Cromwell in 1652, and Claverhouse, the Viscount Dundee stayed there before the Battle of Killecrankie in 1689. The present resident, the Duke of Atholl, has the expensive honour of being the only British subject permitted to retain a private army, the Atholl Highlanders. He also has the dubious honour of contesting the Minigaig's claim to be a right of way despite the fact that it's been used as such for some 400 years!

Diana's Grove, a dark wood of largely foreign conifers celebrating an equally foreign goddess, marks the way to Old Blair, where a track strikes off in a north-west direction beside the Banvie Burn. This track climbs gently through dense woods of birch, larch and pine, keeping in sight of the chuckling burn, which passes through a series of cascades, pools and deep-set ravines, all darkly shaded in bottle green. After a short time, the Rumbling Bridge is reached, a stone hump-back of a bridge which was built in 1762 and bears witness to the fact that the Banvie Burn can, in spate, turn into such a vociferous stream that it actually rumbles the stones and rocks in its river-bed.

Neither the Minigaig nor Comyns Road crosses this bridge, but jointly march forward through a gate into the Whim Plantation before splitting at another gate which marks the end of the woods. Comyns Road stretches onwards, while the Minigaig drops down to the burnside where it crosses the Quarry Bridge, built eight years after the Rumbling Bridge from stones taken from the quarry a few hundred yards upstream.

It was good to walk out of the gloominess of the woods and on to the sun-soaked Banvie moors. Clear of the trees, the landscape changes dramatically. Above the track a series of zigzags on the slope indicated the old path once used by peat cutters fetching their turf from Tom nan Cruach, 'the hillock of peat stacks'.

Soon the track, known locally as the West Hand Road, begins to incline as it pulls away from Glen Banvie up the glen of the Allt na Moine Bàine towards a tall pile of stones, the Lady March Cairn. Apparently, in the nineteenth century Lady March built a small cairn during a picnic lunch, and, as is the way with indiscriminate cairn-building, some workmen, supposed to be repairing the West Hand Road nearby, later added to the cairn until it was over six feet in height. Like a dog leaving its scent, man also seems to have a desire to leave his mark, however inappropriate – a precursor of modern graffiti, I suppose.

Beyond the cairn the road crosses the Allt na Moine Bàine and skirts around the long open slopes of Carn Dearg Beag to drop into the shallow valley of the Allt ant-Seapail, 'the stream of the chapel'. Just after the old trackside stone which marks the three-mile milestone there is a fine old circular well by the name of Fuaran Bhadenoch, another indication of this old road's antiquity and its ultimate destination.

It's also about here that the line of the original Minigaig leaves the more modern West Hand Road for a short distance to meander across the eastern slopes of Meall Dubh. Some four or five miles into the walk I was beginning to get into the swing of things, the pack settling with little creaks and groans, the first sweats broken, and for the first time an opportunity to look around as I walked along. By now, the low winter sun had flooded the broad slopes with its brittle radiance, spilling its long tentacle-like shadows into every scoop and hollow, in a chequerwork of black and gold. Far and wide under the infinity of the domed sky the land stretched away, yellow deer grasses bright and intense in colour, with every feature picked out and etched by the smile of the low sun, ridge over ridge, horizon over horizon, rolling moors and shadow-stained glens, clear-cut land and glistening water.

I passed another large cairn, the Carn Mhic Shimidh, this one a memorial to a battle between the Murrays of Atholl and a raiding party of Frasers led by Simon Lovat. The cairn marks the spot where Lovat was slain. Not far from the cairn the old path meets up with the West Hand Road again for its final stretch to the bothy beside the Allt Sheicheachan.

Dawdling at the lovely Allt Scheicheachan bothy for a brew, I had a look at the map and tried to work out a rough timetable. It was now after midday, and if I was going to try to get across the high pass of the Minigaig before dark I couldn't afford to dawdle too much. On the other hand, if I decided to camp on this side of the pass I would be setting up camp before three o'clock, which would mean a long, long night in the tent. It was also likely that the weather would change overnight and I would be faced with the climb over the watershed on the following day in what could be miserable conditions. So with the sun shining and a good track in front of me, I decided to try to get over the high ground and into Coire Bhran on the Tromie side of the pass before camping. That would leave me with a fairly easy walk down Glen Tromie on the next day, skirting over the low ridge of Sron na Gaoithe and down to Ruthven.

Gulping down my caffeine fix, I packed up the stove and set off, thinking that the soldiers and drovers of old, who used this route just as we use the A9 over the Drumochter Pass today, probably faced the same uncertainties. There was one major

ABOVE: THE DECEMBER SUN WASN'T GOING TO DIE WITHOUT A FINAL FLOURISH, TURNING THE SNOW ON
THE HIGH, PEATY PLATEAU OF THE MINIGAIG PASS TO VARIOUS SHADES OF PINK.

RIGHT: THE ROUTE APPEARS AS MERE TRACINGS OVER THIS BROAD, UPHEAVED BLANKET. TO THE WEST, THE
PEAKS HAD SUNK AND DWINDLED INTO A DISTANT HORIZON AND IN THEIR PLACE THIS GREAT PLATEAU SPREAD
ITSELF AIMLESSLY, A LOFTY TABLELAND PATCHED IN THE BLACK AND WHITE OF PEAT HAGS AND SNOW.

FAR RIGHT: THE LADY MARCH CAIRN IN THE GLEN OF THE ALLT NA MOINE BÀINE, JUST NORTH OF BLAIR
ATHOLL. ACCORDING TO LOCAL LEGEND, ONE LADY MARCH BUILT A CAIRN HERE IN THE NINETEENTH
CENTURY DURING A PICNIC LUNCH.

•

difference though. Up until this century little movement took place between settlements during the months of winter, and traffic over the Minigaig would have been
minimal during the short days of December. The Highlanders of old had more sense
than modern backpackers, particularly modern solo backpackers.

Most people prefer company, and by every reasonable standard of thought they are
absolutely correct. It's been said that for efficiency and comfort and the rewards of
sharing, and above all for safety, a walking party, like a political party, should consist of
at least two or three members, but there are times when I like, indeed I prefer, to be
alone – when trying to regulate thoughts about writing a book like this, when I feel the
need to contemplate my feeble input into this great universe they call creation,
or when I want simply to contemplate that creation itself. Or when I'm fed up, bored,
disgusted, disappointed or feel rejected by people. Wilderness backpacking then
becomes a therapy rather than a test, and that therapy, like much remedial treatment,
is personal, and is best sought alone.

The burn outside the bothy was easily forded, and although much of the path was
now virtually a watercourse I trudged through the deep, clagging heather at the side
around the foot of Druim Dubh and into Glen Bruar.

At the beginning of the last century, Glen Bruar was described as follows: 'About
eight miles north of Blair Atholl, you descend into a glen which is wild and desolate.
The heather being old is rather of a brown than a purple colour, but there is some relief
of greensward near the lodge and more in various patches near the winding source of
the Bruar. At the right of the entrance to the pass, the lonely dwelling called Bruar
Lodge lies a mere speck beneath Ben Dearg. Down winds the Bruar through the glen,
sometimes creeping silently through the mossy stones, at others raving maddening and
bearing it all before it. Nearby, in front of the lodge is a wooden footbridge raised high
above the water, so as to give it a free passage. Some distance up the glen, towards the
east, a lofty cataract falls from the mountainside and the head of the glen is obstructed
by a chain of mountains.'

Nearly 200 years later that description is still accurate. The track up the glen is now
wider, although it's on the opposite side of the river to the Minigaig and the slopes
show the irregular patchwork markings of seasonal heather burnings, but the Lodge
still stands as a speck below Beinn Dearg, the lofty cataract still falls from the hillside
and the end of the glen is still obstructed – by some steep hills rather than the more
fanciful chain of mountains.

Past the rather dilapidated-looking lodge, the end of Glen Bruar abuts on to the
steep face of Uchd a' Chlàrsair, or 'brow of the harper', and the fast, loose rhythm of
the walk up the glen is exchanged for the slower tread up the steep slope. The character of the walk changes dramatically too, as the wide open skies above this vast upland
plateau contrast with the past few miles of hemmed-in glen.

It was now that I began to hesitate a little, in some degree perhaps because my childhood bogeys were not quite dead in me, but mainly because the way ahead was no more than a suggestion, sporadically marked by tiny cairns across a landscape that refused to conform to any accepted pattern. Ahead of me, across this broad upheaved blanket, lay the mere tracings of the old route, much of it obscured by vast swaths of snow. To the north and to the west, the peaks and tops had sunk and dwindled into a distant horizon, and in their place this great plateau spread itself aimlessly, a lofty tableland patched in the black and white of peat hags and snow.

This was like no normal pass which rises to a summit and then immediately descends. For no less than three miles the vast upland of hillocks and brows rolled on, serried knolls which apparently stretched onwards into infinity. Owing to the peculiar configurations of the surrounding landscape, where the ground falls away gently towards bigger hills in the east and lifts imperceptibly northwards to the great desolation of the watershed which leads to the upper Coire Bhran, there seemed to be no end in view, and it was now after three o'clock. In just over an hour it would be dark.

Despite the uncertainty I was captivated by the place. I stood and stared long at the still and silent spread of it, inimical under the increasingly long shadows of the dying winter sun. I recalled the tales of the sithens, the fairly knolls, and remembered the ill fame of the place. Like nearby Gaick, the Minigaig had a particularly bad reputation having claimed many victims by the uncertainty of its weather on this storm-swept plateau. I recalled the words of the modern guidebook I had scorned earlier…

Three miles over the plateau and I was able to drop down into Coire Bhran just as the winter darkness was falling. An hour or so descending a sketchy path by the light of a headtorch took me down the length of the corrie to a fine camping spot by the river, where I settled down for a quiet night, content with a good meal, a book and a dram or two.

I love these long, dark winter nights in a tent, but I'm only too aware that not everyone shares this curious passion. Some people, even keen hill folk, simply don't like the dark, and it is amazing how many can experience all the bleaker manifestations of the unknown when the lights go out! I'm not talking here about the sodium-induced half-darkness of our cities at night, but real darkness – black of night stuff, an intense Cimmerian blackness which can vividly feed the imagination. And that can be a very real barrier to the enjoyment of wilderness backpacking. I've known of folk who have ventured out into the wild places – folk who have planned their trip and looked forward to it and dreamed about it for months – only to pack up and turn tail when faced with the stark reality of the dark unknown.

My little nook by the stream was only a couple of miles from the point where Comyns Road and the Minigaig join together, at the foot of the Gaick Pass at Glen Tromie. On all sides of these broad straths the hills rise to over 2000 feet (610 m), steep sided and smooth, perfect examples of potential avalanche slopes. Drifting clouds of snow blow across the flat plateaux during the winter and pile up in the lee

NEARING JOURNEY'S END. THE TRACK CROSSES THE SPINE OF LAND BETWEEN GLEN TROMIE AND STRATHSPEY TO RUN DOWN TO THE BADENOCH VILLAGE OF KINGUSSIE.

•

side of the slope, in great depths, just waiting for someone, or something, to trigger them off. It was probably an avalanche which caused one of Gaick's best-known supernatural happenings.

In January 1800 Black John MacPherson of Ballachroan took four companions on a shooting expedition to Gaick. As an erstwhile recruiting officer, MacPherson was not a particularly popular person in the area, hence his name, Black John. The weather was ferocious, with strong winds and drifting snow, but he ridiculed the warnings of his friends, who told him he was crazy going off in such weather. The nights were spent in a hut close to where the present Gaick Lodge stands, and one night a bright fire was spotted burning high on the summit of the hill above them. This was seen as a bad omen, and once again Black John was advised to quit the expedition and go home. He disagreed, and several days later the hut was found destroyed, torn to shreds by some powerful, malevolent force. Black John and those companions who had stayed with him were all found dead in the vicinity. The annihilation, so sudden and complete, was put down to supernatural causes, although it's now generally believed that a huge avalanche was the power which destroyed the hut and its occupants. No one, though, has yet put forward a theory to explain the mysterious fire.

The lonely miles of Glen Bruar with Bruar Lodge in the distance. The Minigaig follows the glen to the distant hills before it climbs abruptly to cross its high pass northwards.

•

Coire Bhran to Kingussie

•

I churned these thoughts through my mind as I packed up in the morning. The anticipated storm hadn't happened, but the fine weather had been replaced by a dour, grey drizzle. On such mornings it's best to just get on with it. After following the river for a mile or so I came across a bulldozed track, which eventually joined up with the tarmac road that runs up the length of Glen Tromie to Gaick Lodge. A keeper was mending a fence and jumped with a start when I bade him good morning.

An old Gaelic bard once described Glen Tromie as 'Gleann Tromaidh nan Siantan', 'the glen of the stormy blasts', and in the depths of winter, when the bare birches are cold and grey against the snow-covered ground, and the sky above has that heavy menace of a winter storm, then that description just about sums it up. Things are better at other times of the year, though, with birch, alder and juniper decorating the river-banks. After the starkness of the higher reaches of the Minigaig, the calmness and tranquillity of Glen Tromie is a delight.

About a mile past the old Bhran Cottage, nowadays used as a storage hut by the estate, a narrow bridge took me across the river, from where I wandered past some ancient settlements before starting the long ascent of Sron na Gaoithe, 'the nose of the winds'. There's a prominent cairn on this slope, marked on the map as Carn Pheigith, 'Peggy's cairn'. Tradition has it that this mound of stones marks the burial place of one Peggy, a suicide of the fourteenth century. At that time heaps of stones were traditionally erected over the graves of the dead to secure the remains from the predations of wolves. It became customary to toss another stone on top as you passed by, hence the proverb, Were I dead, you wouldn't throw a stone on it, meaning, you obviously don't think too much of me!

It's a gentle climb over the Sron, and as you pass the crest of the ridge the views open up northwards in vast scale. The twin villages of Newtonmore and Kingussie, separated only by three miles and a hundred years of intense shinty rivalry, nestle under the great swell of the Monadhliath, and here and there a tell-tale splash of water showed where the River Spey meandered through its vast flood-plains. The track can be seen easily from here, picking its way over the heather slopes towards the small crest of Beinn Bhuidhe, a delightful climax to the walk. With big views to the north and to the west, it was only a matter of time before the high tops of the Cairngorms came into view in the east, wreathed in the grey-white of fresh snowfall.

It wasn't long before the scrubby winter heather gave way to short-cropped turf, with sandy rabbit-infested embankments. A couple of gates took me past some more ruins before the biggest ruin of the old township of Ruthven came into view, the gaunt, fire-destroyed walls of Ruthven Barracks. General Wade constructed the building for his dragoons on the same prehistoric mound which Comyn had used in the thirteenth century, and which Fionn MacCumhail, or Fingal, had allegedly used way back in the very mists of time. Wade's building had a short life-span though: some twenty-five years, before being burnt down in 1746 on the orders of Charles Edward Stuart on the run from Culloden.

It's only a mile and a half or so to Kingussie by the minor road that runs below the interminable roar of the A9 – the latest, and without doubt the least attractive, of all the roads through the eastern Grampians.

CHAPTER FIVE

LETTEREWE

THE GREAT WILDERNESS

•

Richard Else

A three-day walk through the Letterewe, Fisherfield and Strathnasheallag Forests

---

MAP: *OS 1:50 000 Sheet 19*

START: *Incheril, just off the A832. Grid Ref: 035621*

FINISH: *Dundonnell Hotel, on the A832. Grid Ref: 090880*

LENGTH: *32 miles (51 km)*

APPROXIMATE TIME: *3 days*

TERRAIN: *A remote walk with no easy way out of the Letterewe wilderness, so you need to make sure you are entirely self-sufficient*

ACCOMMODATION: *Plenty of hotels, guest-houses and two campsites at Gairloch. However, for a taste of real comfort the Dundonnell Hotel is conveniently situated at the end of the walk and serves superb food in both its restaurant and bar*

MEALS: *A variety of establishments in Gairloch, but very limited choice at either end of the walk – check carefully if you are undertaking this walk outside the tourist season. Kinlochewe has a very friendly café serving basic but well-cooked food*

TRANSPORT: *Westerbus runs a service on Tuesday, Thursday and Friday between Aultbea and Inverness, which enables people to travel between Kinlochewe and Gairloch. On Monday, Wednesday and Saturday the service runs between Gairloch and Inverness via Dundonnell. My experience is that they are extremely helpful to walkers and will stop at most reasonable places*

The very name Letterewe has a magical, almost a sacred quality in the eyes of many hill-walkers. This is due to many factors, not least the inaccessibility of this region, its sheer size and its tremendously varied scenery. If I had to settle for just one wilderness area in Britain, this would almost certainly be it.

What most hill-goers call simply Letterewe is an area of approximately a hundred square miles. It is conveniently bounded by the A832 on its southern, western and northern sides as the road threads its way from Kinlochewe to Gairloch, onwards to

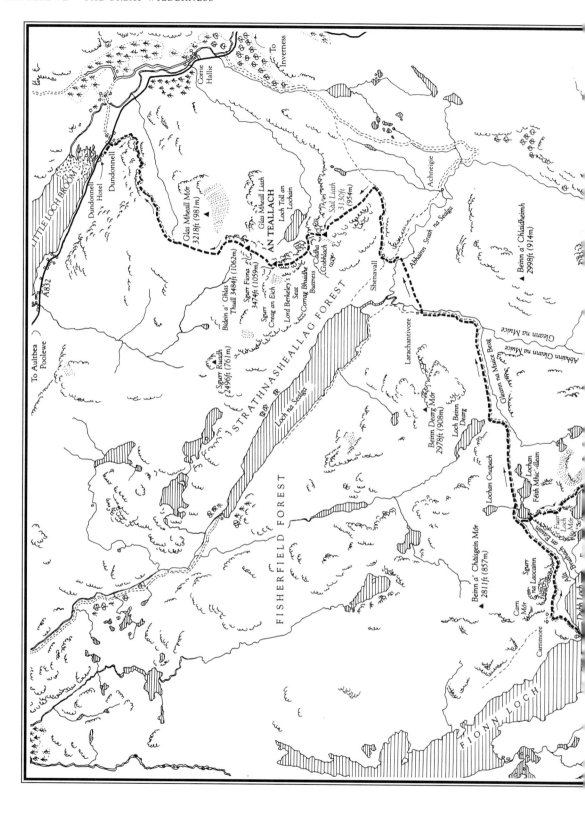

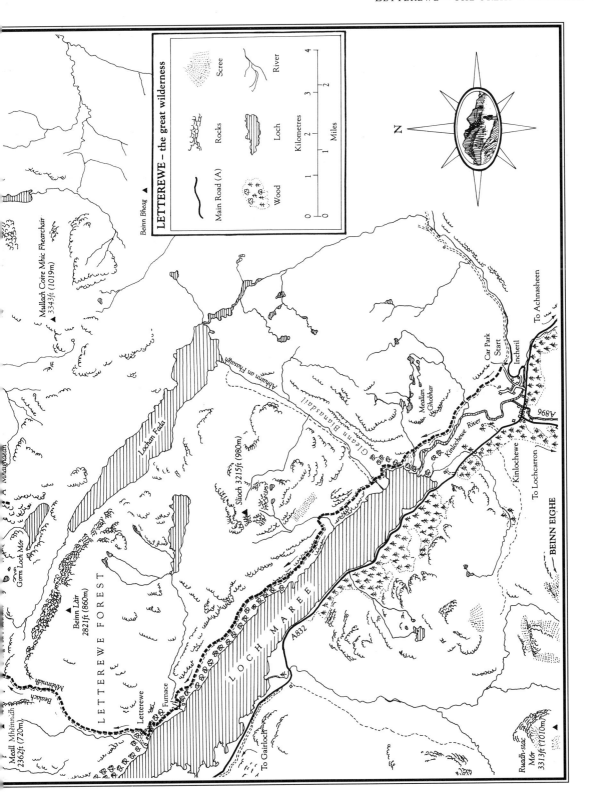

LETTEREWE – the great wilderness

Scree

River

Rocks

Loch

Kilometres

Miles

Main Road (A)

Wood

Beinn Bheag ▲

Mullach Coire Mhic Fhearchair
3343ft (1019m) ▲

To Achnasheen

Car Park
Start

Incheril

Meallan
Ghobhar

Kinlochewe River

A896

Kinlochewe

To Lochcarron

BEINN EIGHE

Lochan Fada

Abhainn an Fhasaigh

Sgùrr Bàn

Sloch 3215ft (980m) ▲

Gleann Bianasdail

LOCH MAREE

A832

Gorm Loch Mòr

A' Mhaighdean

Beinn Lair
2821ft (860m) ▲

LETTEREWE FOREST

Letterewe

Furnace

Meall Mhèinnidh
2362ft (720m) ▲

Bealach
Mhèinnidh

To Gairloch

Ruadh-stac
Mòr
3313ft (1010m) ▲

Poolewe and then around the coast to Dundonnell. On the eastern side the area is separated from another fine walking area, the Fannaichs, by a somewhat arbitrary line running northwards up Gleann Tanagaidh, over Beinn Bheag and east of the Abhainn Gleann na Muice river.

To complicate matters a little further, the region that most walkers refer to simply as the Letterewe wilderness comprises Letterewe Forest, Fisherfield Forest and Strathnasheallag Forest. So what is the attraction of Letterewe and why do walkers rate it so highly?

Certainly it is the largest wilderness area in Britain, but then size isn't everything; arguably it is also the most remote, but then sheer isolation of itself does not make for greatness. To my mind, the real attraction of Letterewe is the enormous variety of the scenery, some of which compares with the finest mountain landscapes in Europe. This is a bold claim when even the highest mountain, An Teallach, is on a small scale compared with such giants as Mont Blanc and the Matterhorn. But the sheer variety of scenery in this area is what wins the day for me. Whether it's wild camping in Slioch's high corrie during a late, but fierce, May snowstorm, or watching, from a high vantage point above Dubh Loch, the sun setting over Fionn Loch and Beinn Airigh Charr, this is a landscape of very special qualities. I hope I am not simply a masochist but the 'long walk in' needed to reach the very heart of Letterewe makes such memories even more precious. I cannot stumble into Letterewe; I need carefully to plan each trip knowing that by the time you reach its heart the weather may have changed. Almost certainly I will have realized I could have been more fit, but that like any longer expedition, be it to the Alps or Himalayas, I will in some way have been changed by the experience. Which for me at least is the whole point of walking in the wilderness.

But all of this is to race ahead. For this walk I entered Letterewe from the small but attractive hamlet of Incheril just outside Kinlochewe. Here a few whitewashed cottages, farm buildings and the local school share a splendid situation in a plain formed by the Kinlochewe River. Now there is a new large car-park, which undoubtedly reflects the influence of the Munro-baggers, and like all car-parks it seems to have generated its own increase in traffic. Here earnest long-distance backpackers mingle with mountain-bike enthusiasts who, in turn, are joined by families out for a short day's walk. I park the Land Rover and pull out all the paraphernalia for my trip, knowing that every ounce has to be carried with me for the next three days and that there is a compromise between, on the one hand, taking everything you think you *just* might need and regretting most of it after the first few hours and, on the other hand, the spartan approach of carrying very little and making do. I favour the latter, although I think it is still possible to manage with even less. Incidentally, Cameron pretends to follow this line, but his idea of what is essential usually includes a least two bottles from the local off-licence! He says any fool can be uncomfortable; I call it lack of will-power, but if he offers to share any of his liquid I accept simply to be sociable.

When I made this trip, in summer, Cameron and I had, on previous walks, been debating the concept of lightweight backpacking and I thought it would be fascinating to see exactly what I thought *was* essential (as opposed to what I claimed to Cameron), so I made a detailed list and then weighed the resulting pack. Now you can take this little game to extremes – for example, is one rucksack lighter than another? – but the Letterewe walk brings a certain amount of common sense to bear because the consequences of getting things wrong can be, at best, inconvenient; at worst they can be disastrous.

Into my rucksack went a shell top and overtrousers, hat and gloves. At this stage I was wearing my fleece, so that was the clothing done. I also added the lightest, if not the most comfortable, tent I had, which weighed in at just 3 pounds (1 ½ kg); the obligatory closed cell foam mat (lighter though less comfortable than the modern inflatable mattress) and a two-season down sleeping-bag. For cooking I had a lightweight stove with its own small pan, so I added another billy pan; a knife, fork and spoon set together with a plastic cup; a Swiss army knife; spare fuel and priming paste and exactly enough dehydrated food for my three days. The latter was minimal, with hot cereal to start; soup and main meals for the evening; chocolate and similar snacks for lunch stops; and coffee and powdered milk.

What I euphemistically called 'luxuries' comprised a camera with three rolls of film. In total, the sack weighed a shade under 22 pounds (10 kg) and sat easily on my shoulders. I left the car-park with a feeling of satisfaction. Cameron may have his wine and goodies, but I was down to this, and happy enough with it.

Incheril to Fionn Loch

•

Whether you enter Letterewe from Incheril, from Poolewe in the west or from near Dundonnell in the north matters not – it is still a long walk in! As I strolled along the track under Meallan Ghobhar towards Gleann Bianasdail and the bridge crossing over the Abhainn an Fhasaigh there was little time for idle musing. To the south were dramatic views towards Beinn Eighe and the Torridon mountains, immediately surrounding me was the river plain with the gorse bushes in full bloom, and further ahead the tip of Loch Maree. I was also looking out for the remains of the iron industry which in the seventeenth century gave rise to a number of thriving settlements on the northern side of Loch Maree. They were known as 'bloomeries': this is the name given to the first forge through which the metal passes after it has been melted from the ore. At this stage the metal is made into 'blooms', or ingots. You can trace these settlements by the many ruins you see while walking up the side of the loch (and which are far more numerous than the 1:50 000 OS map would suggest) and

ABOVE: A TANTALIZING GLIMPSE INTO THE 'GREAT WILDERNESS'. THE VIEW
LOOKING NORTH-EAST ACROSS LOCH MAREE TO THE ISOLATED BULK OF SLIOCH, THE SPEAR. BEYOND IT
LIE LETTEREWE, FISHERFIELD AND STRATHNASHEALLAG, WITH HILLS THAT CAN ONLY BE REACHED BY
'THE LONG WALK IN'.

LEFT: THE TIERED CLIFFS OF BEINN LÀIR FROM THE ROCKY SLOPES OF A' MHAIGHDEAN, THE MAIDEN.

•

by names such as 'furnace'. At the height of the iron industry, tons of trees were felled every year. Just one example will serve to give a sense of scale: the Red Smiddy furnace alone used some 300 acres of trees every year and it was in operation for some sixty years. No wonder this 'forest' is now one in name only.

It is hard to imagine, but this northern side of Loch Maree was once the only line of communication westwards, and before Ullapool evolved as a fishing port in the last century this was the main route between the Western Isles and Inverness. Osgood Mackenzie, writing in *A Hundred Years in the Highlands*, recalls the exploits of Iain Mor am Posda, otherwise known as Big John the Post, who brought the mail and newspapers to these remote communities. With his small home-made leather bag, 'he trudged, I might say climbed, through the awful precipices of Creag Thairbh (the Bull's Rock) on the northern side of Loch Maree, passing through Ardlair and Letterewe, and so on at one time to Dingwall, but latterly only to Achnasheen. Imagine the letters and newspapers for the parish of Gairloch and Torridon, with about 6000 souls, and the Lews [by which he meant the Isle of Lewis], with a population of nearly 30 000 inhabitants, all being carried on one man's back!' Indeed, it had been Osgood Mackenzie's own mother who, during the potato famine of 1846–8, had declared that no one should starve on their property and organized the building of the present road on the southern side of the loch to give the men meaningful work.

Later in the day, easily eating up the eight miles between Incheril and Letterewe, I started thinking about the recent history of this great estate. At one time Letterewe had been a busy hamlet, with its own school for the children of estate workers, but in recent years it has been the home of Paul Van Vlissingen. His attitude to walkers and climbers was, initially, less than favourable, and a number of Keep Out notices appeared around the estate. As you would expect, this caused consternation among outdoor organizations and, perhaps surprisingly, to another member of the aristocracy, John Mackenzie. John has a series of titles, including Earl of Cromartie and Clan Chief of the Mackenzies, but among climbers he is known as the author of the Scottish Mountaineering Club's guide *Rock & Ice Climbs in Skye*. He was incensed that access to the Letterewe estate, with its famous crags like Carn Mór, might be in jeopardy and said so publicly. What appeared in one newspaper was a story stating that he would organize a mass trespass of his clan on Van Vlissingen's land! That march never happened, but what did follow was two years of detailed debate involving not just Mackenzie and Van Vlissingen but also representatives of numerous bodies, including the Ramblers' Association and the Mountaineering Council of Scotland.

It is worth recalling this incident in some detail because the result of all this deliberation and, according to John, some excellent hospitality from Van Vlissingen was the publication in 1993 of *The Letterewe Accord*. The importance of the accord is not simply in what it says, although it does guarantee walkers certain rights and, in return, demands from us a responsible attitude, but in the fact that for the first time anywhere in Britain a landowner has acknowledged that recreational users, to use a bit of jargon, have rights to roam over his land. In my view, this is not the end of the matter but an extremely encouraging beginning. We feel that the accord is of such significance that we have decided to include the whole of its text exactly as written: see pages 93–4.

The accord will need careful monitoring and perhaps revising in the light of experience. At the time of writing some of the original unfriendly signs still need to be replaced, but every walker should thank Paul Van Vlissingen for taking such a bold step. And other landowners should perhaps think about what they can learn from this relative newcomer's attitude.

Leaving the car-park at Incheril in late morning meant that I had missed other walkers, but it also meant that I had to keep up a steady pace to reach my first campsite, which I planned to be high above Dubh Loch and within striking distance of A' Mhaighdean. The gentle walk uphill from Letterewe and over the Bealach Mhèinnidh was a real joy. Behind were attractive views across Loch Maree and its mysterious islands, and ahead I watched a flock of the wild goats that graze throughout Letterewe. But the real bonus came with two eagles soaring high overhead. What a fabulous place, I thought, as I recalled the people I had met on trips here. Nearly all had come to appreciate the special qualities of this landscape, and walking over the bealach provided immediate evidence of them. As the track leads down, you see Fionn Loch spread out beneath and the narrow causeway that separates it from Dubh Loch. Ahead is Carn Mór with the many climbs up its buttress, but to my mind what makes this view so special is its sheer intricacy. What I find so moving about these rocks and lochs is not just the forceful landmarks but the multitude of less obvious but none the less beautiful features dotting this vast panorama. The cliffs of Creag Poll Fraochain (reference 970752) are not marked on the 1:50 000 map, but they form a dramatic backdrop on your right, as do those of Creag an Dubh Loch (reference 982756) further down. Look westwards and there is the northern face of Meall Mhèinnidh (reference 955754), while ahead and to the right of Carn Mór is the towering bulk of Sgurr na Laocainn (reference 985773). But best of all you can see your route ahead sweeping down to the causeway between the two lochs before it heads north-eastwards under Càrnan Bàn.

I arrived here at about half-past five, and for the next few hours was mesmerized by the setting sun bouncing fragments of silver light off both lochs. For most of the time I did not see anyone, not even in the distance, and the feeling of tranquillity and solitude was as profound as any I have felt, be it travelling in arctic Scandinavia or the Himalayan foothills. Later, having traversed the causeway and toiled up the opposite side, I pitched my lightweight tent high on the hill near a small burn and, apart from the roar of my pressurized stove as I cooked in the open, the tranquillity was undisturbed. Even at ten o'clock it was only a feeling of contented weariness that forced me inside and into the sleeping-bag. I have had many perfect mountain days, but this was one of the best – especially the view westwards across Fionn Loch to Skye.

ABOVE: AN TEALLACH IN WINTER SPLENDOUR, THE SNOW EMPHASIZING THE DEEP-CUT GULLEYS AND
PINNACLES OF THIS, ARGUABLY THE MOST IMPRESSIVE MOUNTAIN ON MAINLAND SCOTLAND.
THE PHOTOGRAPH IS TAKEN FROM THE MOUNTAIN'S HIGHEST POINT, BIDEIN A' GHLAS THUILL, LOOKING
TOWARDS THE PINNACLE OF CORRAG BHUIDHE, LORD BERKELEY'S SEAT, AND THE HILLS'
OTHER MUNRO SUMMIT, SGURR FIONA.

RIGHT: LOOKING WEST DOWN THE LENGTH OF LOCH NA SEALGA FROM THE SLOPES OF AN TEALLACH.

A' Mhaighdean to Shenavall

•

A' Mhaighdean, along with its immediate northerly neighbour Ruadh Stac Mór, is usually described as being the most remote Munro, which is probably true (providing you do not confuse remoteness with inaccessibility), but should not blind any walker to the fine qualities of this mountain. If you approach the hill from the east it is an easy but long toil, but taking a western line of ascent is a different matter altogether. Crossing the Allt Bruthach an Easain just as it leaves the Lochan Féith Mhic'-illean, there is a marvellous stalkers' path that weaves upwards between Ruadh Stac Mór and the high, austere Fuar Loch Mór. This path is an impressive construction especially when you step to one side to look at the foundations and ponder on the amount of manpower it must have taken to construct and, in view of its present condition, on the quality of that labour. Above the loch you cross the upland plateau, making a south-westerly track for the summit.

On my recent visit I met a fellow-walker who had been here a year earlier and on that occasion had noticed a Bible placed within the summit cairn. The word of God, on paper at least, had taken a battering in the intervening twelve months and now only a few dishevelled pages remained. Retracing my steps I wondered who had left the book there and why this particular summit? Incidentally, A' Mhaighdean means, as you might expect, 'the maiden', but Peter Drummond, in his enlightening book *Scottish Hill and Mountain Names*, points out that in both Scots and Gaelic cultures a maiden is also the last sheaf of corn cut during the harvest. Many Highland traditions are associated with this last stook when, after a good harvest, it would be dressed to look like a young girl.

From the summit of A' Mhaighdean I retraced my steps on to the plateau between this hill and Ruadh Stac Mór, noticing an abundance of places in which to bivvy and also enjoying sliding down the extensive patches of snow which still remained on this north-facing slope in spite of many days of warm weather. Munro-baggers can take a brief diversion to claim Ruadh Stac Mór before once again joining the stalkers' path on their descent. The path between Carnmore and Shenavall forms a main walkers' artery from the south-west to the north-east of Letterewe. After the exertion involved in gaining the summits, the path provides a delightfully easy way through the wilderness with a most spectacular descent by the southernmost tip of Loch Beinn Dearg through Gleann na Muice Beag. This is particularly powerful when seen towards the end of the day with shafts of sunlight picking out individual crags on the mountainside and giving the whole glen a wonderful atmosphere and haunting beauty. Those of us who do not have the good fortune to be born Scots and who are bereft of the Gaelic should strive to understand the history of landscapes like this one.

However well I get to know individual mountains, glens or seascapes on my walks and travels through Scotland, one or two impressions never change. First, there is the sheer scale of the countryside, closely followed by a beauty that is always changing with the seasons and the years, but which rarely disappoints.

At the end of my second day I set about lighting the stove and, with the first brew under way, pitched my tent with the north-east face of Beinn Dearg Mór darkening in ever-lengthening shadows.

Shenavall to Dundonnell

•

The crossing of both the Abhainn Gleann na Muice and Abhainn Srath na Sealga requires the removal of boots and socks, and although I have always crossed these when the water-levels have been moderate, the rivers can require care after heavy rain or melting snow. Usually, I cross the first river near to Larachantivore and the second almost opposite Shenavall. If you have forded them only when the water has been cold, which can persist until well into summer, it may be a surprise to learn that in high summer the water can be both warm and refreshing. On one spring trip I was mighty glad to get my boots back on and feet warmed up again!

Cameron and I had decided, in the writing of this book, to avoid bringing attention to the many bothies found in remote areas of Scotland. There are a number of reasons for this: many walkers already know where such places are, and there is always the joy of discovering new ones for yourself. Also, there is no guarantee that a particular bothy will be able to provide accommodation and, finally, with a number of bothies coming under increased pressure a little less publicity is no bad thing. However, I am making an exception in the case of Shenavall Bothy (which, in any case, many writers have already mentioned). The building is on property owned by the Hon. Mrs Angus Maclay, and her family are happy to continue the tradition of letting responsible walkers have the use of it. They are less pleased, to put it mildly, about the amount of vandalism that has taken place here in recent years and about the way some so-called 'walkers' leave their refuse, and worse, scattered about. This problem is not unique to Shenavall and affects many other refuges, particularly in the Cairngorms. Many landowners have been less tolerant than the Maclays and simply demolished their buildings to stop further trouble. Surely, if we expect landowners to display more openness and co-operation with hill-users, we too have to do our bit.

I think this walk through Letterewe is a classic, and like all good classics it ends on the highest of notes – an ascent of An Teallach. This is one of Scotland's greatest mountains or, perhaps more accurately, mountain ranges, for An Teallach is not just

one summit. On the top of Sgurr Fiona I met a young man and his partner who had come from Bidein a' Ghlas Thuill. After talking about the superb weather, which is by no means certain on this mountain, he said, 'We're off down. We've done the two Munros, haven't we?' This view, which seems to be gaining popularity with some walkers, to my mind misses the whole aesthetic quality of the mountains and the real spirit of wilderness walking. In my opinion, the whole of the An Teallach ridge is a tremendous mountaineering experience and traversing it from south to north is an outing that many walkers will always treasure. Once you have gained the high ground, the ridge drives you relentlessly forward until you reach the final high point, having clambered over or walked beneath, depending on your competence (and confidence!), a succession of weathered summits and pinnacles.

From Shenavall you follow the path east until an obvious direct line up the nose of Sàil Liath is on your left. From here on it is upwards! The gradient eases towards the top, and after a final push Sàil Liath's summit is reached at 3130 feet (954 m). From

LOOKING SOUTH FROM AN TEALLACH REVEALS BOTH THE SPLENDOUR OF THIS RIDGE
AND A SUPER PANORAMIC VIEW OF THE LETTEREWE WILDERNESS.

•

here you can see some, at least, of the summits and pinnacles lying ahead. There is
now a short descent of approximately a hundred yards before climbing again to Cadha
Gobhlach and a further steep pull up to the end of the Corrag Bhuidhe buttress. It is, I
guess, a testimony to both An Teallach's magnetism as a mountain range and its two
most prominent tops being classified as separate Munros that ever-increasing numbers
of feet have passed this way in the last ten years or so. This can be seen in the
widescale erosion that has affected the sandstone base and the ridge path is now very
insecure in places with numerous loose stones. As I crossed towards Corrag Bhuidhe I
wondered how much longer it would be before the kind of restoration work we see on
lower paths would be necessary here. Or should we simply leave this noble mountain

alone? Would that even be a practical proposal? And how should we preserve our wilderness and that landscape we so love?

An Teallach is, more than most, a mountain that amply repays detailed examination, for within its traverse there are many beautiful nooks and crannies. But even the most cursory of visits should include one of its most famous landmarks, Lord Berkeley's Seat, which is between Corrag Bhuidhe and Sgurr Fiona. From here you get gripping views of the surrounding rock walls and the corrie below.

Judging by the path that runs on the western side of Corrag Bhuidhe, a good many of today's walkers seem to avoid the nearest buttress and take this route until they feel confident to regain the tops. Even if you follow the path to its northern extremity and, in effect, turn back to gain Sgurr Fiona, you can still see the towers that form the famous landmarks on the top of Corrag Bhuidhe. On my most recent visit, in glorious weather but with clouds of mist creeping around the base of the ridge, it was on the summit of Sgurr Fiona (3474 feet/1059 m) that we ran into the crowds – people of all ages and nationalities lured to the top by the path from Dundonnell. This is the second-highest point on An Teallach, but to many walkers its shape, situation and position make it their favourite spot, and it is hard to disagree with that opinion. Sitting in the lunchtime sun, we had tremendous views in all directions. Eastwards we looked deep into the corrie of Toll an Lochain; south we admired the pinnacles and traced our route; to the immediate west was Sgurr Creag an Eich and further away Sgurr Ruadh, while to the north lay our next objective and the highest point of the day.

Bidein a' Ghlas Thuill, at 3484 feet (1062 m), claims the distinction of being the highest point on An Teallach but does so by the merest margin. The 1:25 000 OS map puts the difference at two metres, while for some reason that I am not clear about there is a margin of three metres on the 1:50000 map. Either way, it's a close call! Clambering down from Sgurr Fiona and across to Bidein a' Ghlas Thuill is straightforward, and even after a day's exertions it's surprisingly easy. Once you reach the summit and rest by the triangulation pillar, it is time to look back on your achievement.

Of course, in good weather, and certainly when I was there, no one wants to leave this final summit and head down. There is a choice of routes to Dundonnell depending on whether you take in Glas Mheall Mór or not, but either way nothing can compare with what lies behind. In fact, there is only one consolation and one which, with the use of my plastic card, I exercised. The Dundonnell Hotel is, appropriately, one of Scotland's most hospitable and that's pretty good. The staff always have a sympathetic welcome for walkers, so I threw caution to the wind and checked in. Don't worry about the cost – after thirty-two miles you have deserved it!

There is just one small postscript: over a pint I thought back about my trip through Letterewe and, while I would never miss out on An Teallach, my personal highlight was that first night camping above Fionn Loch and that sense of true wilderness and beauty. Height alone does not equal excellence. I wonder if the Munro-baggers realize this?

The Letterewe Accord

•

Some of the finest mountain scenery in Europe is found on the Letterewe Estate in Wester Ross. It is renowned among hillwalkers and climbers for its wild land qualities. The Letterewe Accord is a set of principles whose aim is to enhance public awareness of wild land needs and to provide a guide to its use and enjoyment, both on Letterewe and perhaps elsewhere in the Scottish Highlands. The Accord has been drawn up by Letterewe Estate in co-operation with outdoor organization representatives. It has developed from discussions initiated by the Mountaineering Council of Scotland and the Ramblers' Association with the Estate.

Fundamental to the Accord is the recognition that all who visit, or live and work on the land and water of Letterewe, must cherish and safeguard the area's wildlife and beauty. Such places are increasingly rare in a world where the natural environment is under ever growing pressure. A new approach is needed. Co-operation between individual and community interests in the sound management of wild land is one element. It reaffirms that human needs are inseparable from those of the natural world.

• *The prime objective at Letterewe is to maintain, expand and enhance the area's biological diversity and natural qualities. This will ensure that these are central to the experience of all who visit the area and are recognized as an essential element in sustaining the long-term economy of Wester Ross.*
• *Red deer management policy is based on selective culling, aided by scientific research, with the aim of maintaining population levels appropriate to the regneration of the natural habitat.*
• *All who visit the area are asked to recognize that red deer stalking is carried out across most of the estate area with the most important period being weekdays from 15 September to 15 November. Visitors are asked to contact the estate during this period for further advice.*
• *Visitors are encouraged to base their visit to Letterewe on the concept of 'the long walk in'. Adequate experience, training and equipment to meet the rigours of travel in this remote area are essential.*
• *Public use is based on the tradition of freedom of access to all land, subject to any agreed modifications for conservation or management reasons.*
• *There are footpaths through those areas where there are benefits for land management or for visitor access.*
• *Car parking, telephones, etc. are available at Dundonnell, Kinlochewe and Poolewe.*
• *The estate does not favour the construction of new vehicle tracks or the use of all-terrain vehicles. Ponies and boats are used for estate management.*
• *Mountain bikes should be used only on existing roads OR vehicle tracks and not on footpaths or surrounding land.*

THERE HAS BEEN A LONG-STANDING TRADITION OF RESPONSIBLE FREEDOM TO ROAM
IN THE SCOTTISH HIGHLANDS, A TRADITION THAT WAS FIRST FORMALIZED BY THE LETTEREWE ACCORD.

•

• *Minimum-impact techniques should be used when camping overnight using lightweight tents. Pollution and disturbance to wildlife, especially sensitive lochshore birdlife, must be avoided.*
• *Visitors are encouraged to visit the area in small, rather than large groups.*
• *Research studies which help to further understanding of the use and protection of wild land are welcome at Letterewe.*

LETTEREWE ESTATE WILL BE PLEASED TO ADVISE ON ANY ASPECT OF ESTATE
MANAGEMENT AND ON WAYS TO MAKE ANY VISIT TO LETTEREWE AS ENJOYABLE
AND REWARDING AS POSSIBLE

THE LETTEREWE ACCORD
produced by Letterewe Estate in association with John Muir Trust
Mountaineering Council of Scotland
Ramblers' Association Scotland
Scottish Wild Land Group

December 1993

CHAPTER SIX

LETTEREWE

ALONG THE HIGH TOPS

•

Richard Else

A two- to three-day walk in Letterewe Forest's remote eastern mountains

---

MAP: *OS 1:50 000 Sheet 19*
START: *Corrie Hallie, on the A832. Grid Ref: 115852*
FINISH: *Kinlochewe, on the A832. Grid Ref: 027620*
LENGTH: *20 miles (32 km)*
APPROXIMATE TIME: *2–3 days*
TERRAIN, ACCOMMODATION AND TRANSPORT: *See Letterewe – the great wilderness*

This route involves twenty miles of walking taking a north–south line through Letterewe, and although it makes an ideal partner to the ascent of A' Mhaighdean and An Teallach described in the preceding chapter, it is also a wonderful trip in its own right.

It is important to understand that this more easterly route through the Letterewe wilderness is by no means a second choice. On the contrary it consists of an exhilarating traverse taking in three high tops and providing a quite different view of this landscape. And I will also explain how you can easily get back to your car at the end of it all.

I took my fifteen-year-old son James with me on this two- to three-day expedition. I find that both travelling alone or with a companion can be equally enjoyable, although the experience of each is quite different. Often I prefer to travel alone, reflecting in a solitary way on the scenery. On the other hand, a sympathetic companion brings a whole new aspect to the journey. James proved not only the ideal traveller but, on this particular trip, a source of great moral support. We did this walk in what was the hottest summer since the blistering heatwave of 1976 (or, according to some views, the best summer since the Second World War), although temperatures in Wester Ross were slightly below those further south.

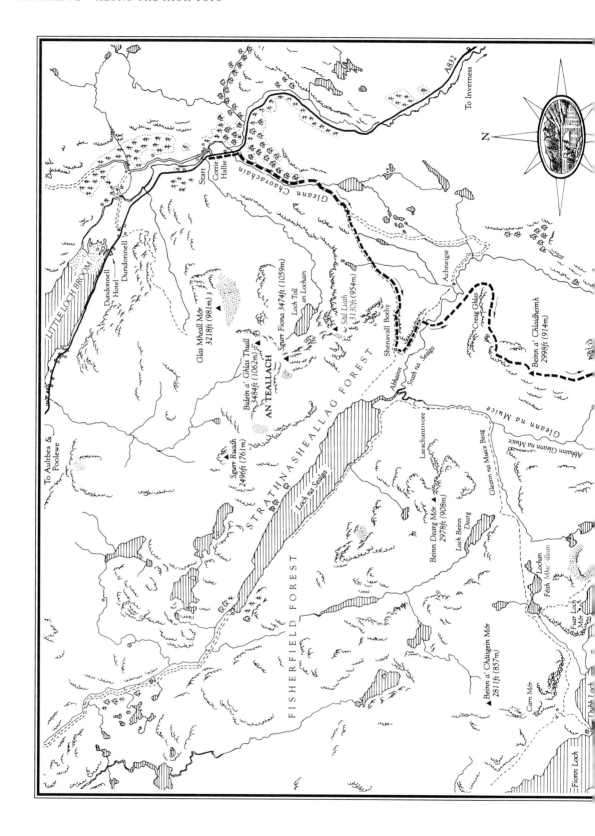

N

To Inverness

A832

Gleann Chaorachain

Start

Corrie Hallie

Achneigie

LITTLE LOCH BROOM

Dundonnell
Hotel

Dundonnell

Glas Mheall Mór
3218ft (981m)

Bidein a' Ghlas Thuill
3484ft (1062m)

Sgurr Fiona 3474ft (1059m)

Loch Toll
an Lochain

Sàil Liath
3130ft (954m)

Creag Ghlas

Beinn a' Chlaidheimh
2998ft (914m)

AN TEALLACH

Shenavall Bothy

Abhainn

Srath na Sealga

Gleann na Muice

STRATHNASHEALLAG FOREST

Sgurr Ruadh
2496ft (761m)

To Aultbea &
Poolewe

Larachantivore

Abhainn Gleann na Muice

Gleann na Muice Beag

Loch na Sealga

FISHERFIELD FOREST

Beinn Dearg Mór
2978ft (908m)

Loch Beinn
Dearg

Lochan
Fèith Mhic-'illean

Fuar Loch
Mór

Beinn a' Chàisgein Mór
2811ft (857m)

Carn Mór

Fionn Loch

Dubh Loch

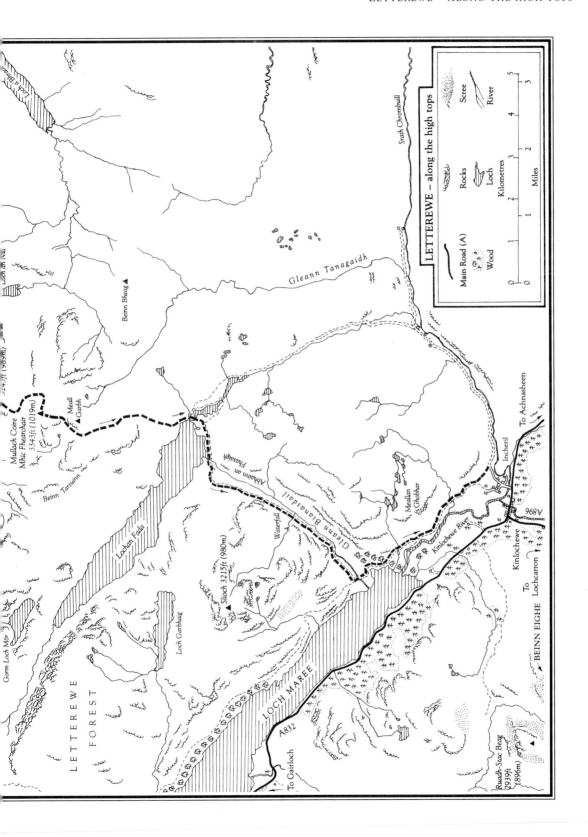

LETTEREWE – along the high tops

Main Road (A)
Wood
Rocks
Loch
Scree
River

Miles
Kilometres

To Achnasheen
Incheril
A896
Kinlochewe
Kinlochewe River
To Lochcarron
BEINN EIGHE

Ruadh-Stac Beag
2939ft
896m

LOCH MAREE
A832
To Gairloch

LETTEREWE FOREST

Gorm Loch Mòr
Loch Garbhaig
Sloch 3215ft (980m)
Waterfall
Abhainn an Fhasaigh
Gleann Bianasdail
Meallan
&Ghobhar
Gleann Tanagaidh
Srath Chrombuill

Lochan Fada
Meall Garbh
Mullach Coire
Mhic Fhearchair
3343ft (1019m)
Beinn Tarsuinn
Benn Bheag
Loch an Nid

ABOVE: THIS MAGNIFICENT VIEW IS THE ONE WHICH GREETS ALL WALKERS AS THEY HEAD SOUTH
TOWARDS LETTEREWE. WHILE BEINN DEARG MÓR DOMINATES THE HORIZON, MANY A WALKER HAS BEEN
GRATEFUL FOR THE ACCOMMODATION PROVIDED BY SHENAVALL BOTHY. SADLY, IN RECENT YEARS,
THIS TRADITIONAL REFUGE HAS SUFFERED FROM OVERUSE.

RIGHT: LOOKING UP THE LENGTH OF GLEANN AN NID WITH SGURR BÀN AND MULLACH COIRE MHIC
FHEARCHAIR TO THE RIGHT. FROM THIS POINT THE PATH DROPS DOWN TO SHENAVALL.

•

Corrie Hallie to Beinn a' Chlaidheimh

•

We left our car in the usual place at Corrie Hallie, but if you have been based at the Dundonnell Hotel then it is a two-mile walk south along the road (unless you can beg a lift from a fellow-guest). In any event, you follow the obvious track that begins alongside the Gleann Chaorachain and which rises steadily upwards. After approximately two miles and on an upland plateau, a path forks right from the track. This is the route to follow, and it leads unerringly towards Shenavall. I normally try to avoid walking in such high temperatures, but there was one consolation – the crossing of the Abhainn Srath na Sealga was a delight, with the water unusually warm. What a change from the icy crossings experienced in the melt waters of spring! The river was so denuded of water that crossing almost anywhere was practicable, but without giving it much thought we crossed near the bothy and made our way alongside the river until we were almost opposite Achneigie.

We had started our journey in mid-afternoon and had wanted to get to about this point, with the intention of leaving the main ascent until the relative cool of the following morning. Congratulating ourselves on a splendid walk in, we looked for a suitable site for the tent. Eventually, we found a good vantage spot about 200 feet above the river and not far from a stream that still had some water in it. The evening looked as if it were going to be perfect, and we were excited about trying out a new stove – as a real luxury we had even brought some 'proper' food in addition to the usual freeze-dried packets.

After pitching the tent, we placed the stove on a large, flat boulder to avoid any fire risk and it was then we had the first hint of trouble. There were only one or two to begin with but their numbers quickly increased and then there was simply the infamous black cloud containing what must be millions of them. *Midges!* It is important to stay calm about this, I told James, and in many years of summer walking in Scotland I could count on my hand the number of times it's been truly desperate (as opposed, of course, to being just bloody awful!). I do not want to be alarmist, but this was one of the very worst evenings ever. We did not get to cook our meal, but that was the least of our problems, and without a very effective midge screen in our Terra Nova tent we would not even have been able to stay put. Kevin Howett in his guide *Rock Climbing in Scotland* has given his routes a 'midge rating' of between one and three. On such a scale the monsters we encountered would rate at least ten! It came as little consolation to discover later that Cameron was having problems of his own further south and that both of our bodies looked like textbook pictures of a particularly virulent disease! Also, don't believe any of the so-called miracle cures; in this type of weather endurance is the only solution.

Beinn a' Chlaidheimh to Mullach Coire Mhic Fhearchair

•

Taking down the tent the following morning was no better: it took me three attempts to do so, and even the best midge repellent seemed only to encourage them. So James and I set off with the tent and other bits just thrown into the rucksacks, with the benefit of neither an evening meal nor breakfast and feeling pretty much demoralized. Without mutual encouragement, I feel that both of us, left to our own devices, would have turned back. Together we somehow found enough determination to battle on, and we were both rewarded by the miles ahead – even if I was still scratching over a week later!

We were heading for Beinn a' Chlaidheimh and began our ascent up tussocky grass and heather behind the rocks of Creag Ghlas. On many Scottish mountains it is hard to get a real sense of perspective other than by looking at the map, and this was certainly true of Beinn a' Chlaidheimh. There is an initial long haul up, then the route is less steep until you come beneath the cliffs at reference 069788. Incidentally, it was only here, nearly 1350 feet (400 m) above our disastrous campsite, that we finally said goodbye to all but a few high-altitude cousins of our winged friends. James and I took some consolation from this: any moving of our tent would not have made our situation any better. The whole area was one large disaster zone.

However, our position was getting more bearable, improved, not least of all, by our surroundings. The rock buttresses ahead of us were impressive and we made our way between them up a steep grassy stairway which had more than a passing resemblance to a vertical ladder. The odd bootprint is a reminder that others have gone this way before, but not in sufficient numbers to make anything other than a vague path – which still gives an illusion of a true wilderness area. The exertion is more than worthwhile, and we were soon standing on the summit at 2999 feet (914 m) and, through the summer haze, we could see clearly neighbouring peaks like An Teallach together with the line we were going to take stretching away due south. It was a pity that the more distant peaks were indistinct outlines, but we still got a sense of scale with Gleann na Muice immediately in front of our feet. The summit ridge is narrow in places and I wondered if this had given rise to its name 'hill of the sword' or if, like other hills in these parts whose names are based on weapons, it alluded to events long since forgotten in the mist of history? However, the effort of climbing this hill is not entirely in the ascent. It is a long trudge off Beinn a' Chlaidheimh, and in heading to a depression east of Loch a' Bhrisidh you lose some 850 feet (260 m) of vertical ascent – all of which will need to be regained.

ABOVE: AN TEALLACH, THE FORGE, IN ALL ITS MAGNIFICENT SPLENDOUR, SEEN FROM THE OLD
'DESTITUTION ROAD' BETWEEN BRAEMORE JUNCTION AND DUNDONNELL. THIS IS THE VIEW THAT HAS
INSPIRED GENERATIONS OF HILL-GOERS.
LEFT: BEINN DEARG MÓR AND BEINN DEARG BEAG, WITH THE SERRATED OUTLINE OF AN TEALLACH
BEYOND, FROM THE HIGH SLOPES OF A' MHAIGHDEAN.

•

Two small lochans, unnamed on the 1:50 000 map, sit in the col between Beinn a' Chlaidheimh and Sgurr Bàn. James had suggested these would make a good place for a decent rest. He was right, and with the sun beating down we got out the stove and ate our first proper meal for nearly twenty-four hours while watching a number of young frogs move in and out of the water. And we counted only five midges! We also met our first walker of the day who, travelling light, had already come in from Corrie Hallie early that morning and was thinking that Sgurr Bàn would have to be his last peak before the long walk out again. I certainly didn't envy a long trudge back out in this heat, but there was something other than that. Sometimes we can get only a few hours in the hills and grab what time we can willingly. Tom Patey, mixing climbing with his doctor's practice in Ullapool, was a classic example of that spirit. But if you have a choice, surely the hills are there to be savoured and best repay contemplation. The longer you can stay in them, the more you attune to their mood, spirit and, perhaps most important of all, their grandeur. Or am I being too mystical?

Certainly there was nothing mystical about what lay ahead – just a concerted effort! We now needed to achieve almost 1120 feet (340 m) of ascent before we would get to our next summit, Sgurr Bàn (3245 feet/989 m). The obvious way is to make for the ridge leading up the eastern skyline, but a large amount of loose boulders and rock make this appear unattractive. The reality is not quite so bad. We made a diagonal route towards the ridge, but before reaching our predetermined point we headed straight on and kept to the grass. We therefore avoided the worst of the scree as we made our final pull up to the summit.

You do not need to know a word of Gaelic to guess that Sgurr Bàn, translated, means 'white peak' – you simply have to use your eyes (although it should be added that Gaelic has more than one word meaning 'white' and each one has its own nuance). Here, though, the summit plateau is what amounts to a rocky desert of quartzite with loose boulders keeping us, literally, on our toes at all times. It would be very easy to turn an ankle on such ground, especially in the wet, and the consequences of such a mishap could be very serious indeed. Both of us voted the descent exceptionally tedious. Yet while this range of hills does not have the majesty associated with A' Mhaighdean, there is, nevertheless, a sense of grandeur associated with traversing these tops. You get a quite different sense of Letterewe than from walking further west.

Our final hill that day was also the highest and the most dramatic. At 3343 feet (1019 m), Mullach Coire Mhic Fhearchair tantalizingly translates as 'peak of the corrie of Farquhar's son'. This led me to thinking that we must surely have lost ninety per cent – or even more – of our history, with often only the big events surviving. David Craig, in his superb book *On the Crofters' Trail*, was perhaps only just in time in tracing the descendants of the Highland Clearances and chronicling the life histories that had been passed down by word of mouth from one generation to the next. But who now knows what events had led to the christening of this summit? Who was Farquhar's son and what had he done that a mountain took its name from him?

This hill can be ascended on its northern nose, but we turned east on reaching the col at approximately 2660 feet (810 m) and, making a diagonal track across the northern face, we made for the easterly subsidiary summit at about 3180 feet (970 m). Once again we trudged across and up yet more unstable boulders, but the situation, with views further east to Loch an Nid, made the effort worth while. As befits an afternoon climb and the third mountain of the day, the pull up this ridge is not an arduous one and within a short time we were on the small top. Then a quick walk across the ridge is needed to gain the top of Mullach. The effort is well rewarded.

Weeks of constant high air pressure had reduced the best views to outlines seen through the haze, but this summit was still an outstanding place on which to be in the late afternoon, especially as the mountain gives the impression of dropping away more steeply on its northern and western sides than is actually the case. The descent from the top, away due south, is again a tedious walk, with care being necessary on the many insecure boulders. Everyone develops his own way of dealing with ground like this – personally, I like to get into a balanced rhythm, and while the speed of my descent will never break any records I make steady and secure progress downwards.

You can ascend Meall Garbh, but we had a good reason for not doing so and instead chose the well-defined path that traverses the north-western slope. Having experienced one night of purgatory, James and I were determined to avoid a repeat performance. The best way of achieving this is to remain as high as possible and where we would be sure to catch any breeze. We found the perfect spot between Meall Garbh and the hazy Beinn Tarsuinn. As the minutes went by we became more secure realizing we had outwitted the black menace. Even the five-minute walk to find running water was nothing compared with the relief at not being under constant attack. We got the stove going and were sat outside preparing a feast when two sweating walkers appeared with a cheerful, 'I bet you thought no one would come this way tonight!' In conversation, they explained that they had started out late, having stayed at Shenavall, and their late beginning had been the result of a desperate night caused by the midges. Like war veterans, we swapped stories and they left, both envious of our insect-free zone and clearly in no great hurry to get back to the bothy. We also learnt something else that evening: chicken Kiev, in freeze-dried form, is quite simply the worst packet meal ever produced. But even that seemed not to matter in the great scheme of things.

OVERLEAF: AN UNFAMILIAR VIEW OF SLIOCH, RISING ABOVE LOCHAN FHADA IN THE LETTEREWE FOREST. THIS IS ALL WILD, UNCOMPROMISING LANDSCAPE – A MIXTURE OF GNEISS AND SANDSTONE THAT GEOLOGISTS BELIEVE TO BE AROUND 80 MILLION YEARS OLD.

•

Meall Garbh to Kinlochewe

•

Our final morning began with a delightful, easy descent from our high col straight down to Lochan Fada. After a short break on the pebbly beach, we followed the track around the southern extremity to the entrance to Gleann Bianasdail. Incidentally, it's important to remember that crossing both streams can be difficult – even impossible – in times of spate. This is true of many Highland watercourses and even experienced hill folk have been drowned in recent years. Indeed, what makes Scottish mountain-walking so different from that elsewhere in Britain is its sheer scale and the need for all of us to be aware of the consequences of our decisions.

However, such thoughts did not trouble us on this particular morning as the temperature soared in the high 80s Fahrenheit and the Factor 20 sun cream came out of the rucksack. Gleann Bianasdail has much of interest, with a whole series of waterfalls; and while we did appreciate the fine views, our feet were now firmly set towards Kinlochewe and the café there. We arrived in the early afternoon, and after copious amounts of liquid and food we sat on wooden benches reading newspapers. What luxury!

Our walk had gone exactly to plan, and we had arrived on one of the days when a solitary bus runs to Gairloch. This village has a lovely small bookshop with exceptionally long opening hours, and I spoke to the owner and her friend about a good many things, including Gaelic and the people who were now learning it in these parts. More practically, they volunteered the news that this was the worst summer for midges in living memory. They had closed all the windows and the door, preferring a midge-free sauna to any alternative. 'Even the cat's being driven mad!'

Early next morning the same bus-driver appeared. Taking a northern circuit to Inverness, he picked up assorted walkers, foreign tourists and a local woman with one of the best sheepdogs I have seen in ages. Together we rattled around to Dundonnell and, being in the Highlands, we were dropped right next to our Land Rover at Corrie Hallie – Alisdair and Wester Ross transport making the almost perfect end to a great walk. It was only spoilt by… well, you've guessed it: those insects made even getting into the vehicle a final trial, the end score being Midges 3, Walkers 1.

CHAPTER SEVEN

AROUND LOCH MULLARDOCH

BASHING MUNROS, AGAIN!

•

Cameron McNeish

A three-day high mountain walk around Loch Mullardoch in Ross-shire

---

MAPS: *OS 1:50 000 Sheet 25*

START AND FINISH: *Loch Mullardoch Dam, Glen Cannich. Grid Ref: 228315*

LENGTH: *45 miles (72 km)*

APPROXIMATE TIME: *3 days*

TERRAIN: *Hard mountain walking over a remote landscape*

ACCOMMODATION: *Cannich has b&b and hotel accommodation, plus a youth hostel which is open only during the summer*

It had been a long time since I'd had my breath taken away by such an incredible view. Mountains seemed to roll on endlessly in all directions, the blue shimmering flatness of the Moray Firth stopping the endless flow to the east, the west, characteristically, presenting its bold, jagged outline of the Skye Cuillin. Ben Nevis crouched in the south, dominating all, and it was fun running my eye along the ranges which formed the southern horizon, the Aonachs, the Grey Corries, Loch Treig and then the Ossian hills, largely obstructed by the Creag Meagaidh massif. Surprisingly far to the east, a mere swell on the horizon, the Cairngorms were easily identified by their high snow patches in Coire Cas and Coire an Lochan.

Northwards, the wonderful hills of Strathfarrar seemed closer than they should be in the intense clarity of the air, and in front of them, beyond the dark blue loch, the hills that would keep me company all day long, Carn nan Gobhar, Sgurr na Lapaich, An Riabhachan and An Socach – every one a Munro (see page 12). I hoped to traverse them all the day after tomorrow.

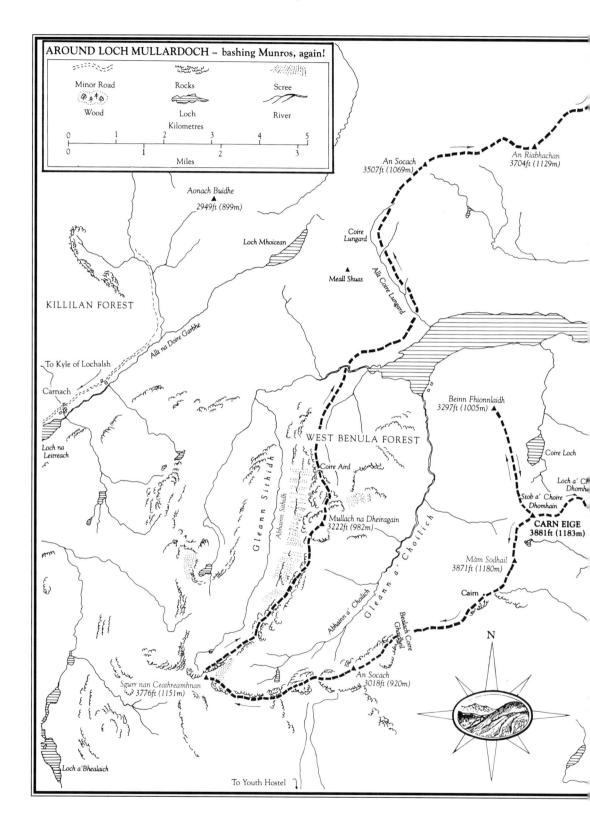

AROUND LOCH MULLARDOCH – bashing Munros, again!

Minor Road

Wood

Rocks

Loch

Scree

River

Kilometres

0   1   2   3   4   5

0   1   2   3

Miles

Aonach Buidhe
2949ft (899m)

An Socach
3507ft (1069m)

An Riabhachan
3704ft (1129m)

Loch Mhoicean

Coire
Lungard

Meall Shuas

Allt Coire Lungard

Beinn Fhionnlaidh
3297ft (1005m)

KILLILAN FOREST

Coire Loch

Allt na Doire Garbhe

To Kyle of Lochalsh

Carnach

Loch a' Ch
Dhomh

Stob a' Choire
Dhomhain

WEST BENULA FOREST

CARN EIGE
3881ft (1183m)

Loch na
Leitreach

Coire Aird

Gleann Sithidh

Abhainn Sithidh

Mullach na Dheiragain
3222ft (982m)

Màm Sodhail
3871ft (1180m)

Cairn

Abhainn a' Choilich

Gleann a' Choilich

Bealach Coire
Ghaidheil

N

Sgurr nan Ceathreamhnan
3776ft (1151m)

An Socach
3018ft (920m)

Loch a'Bhealaich

To Youth Hostel

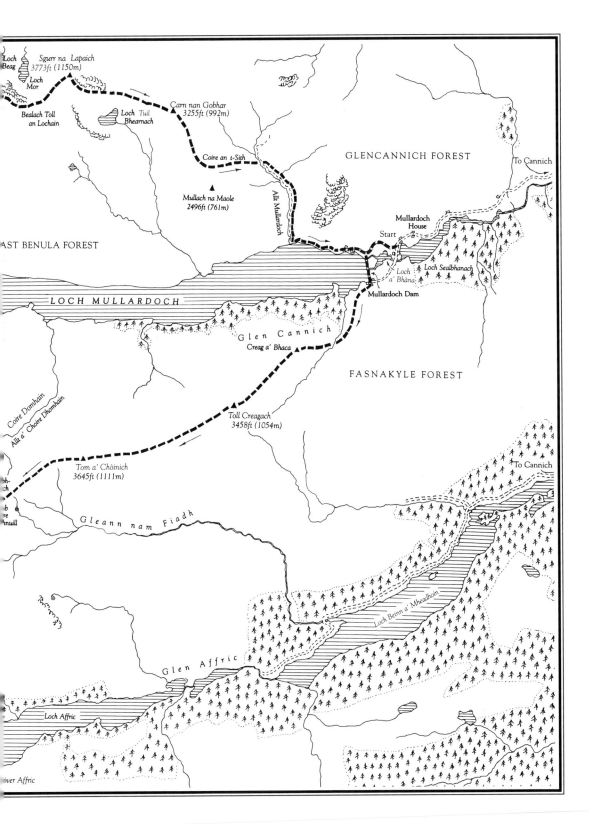

Loch
Beag
Loch
Mor
Sgurr na Lapaich
3773ft (1150m)
Bealach Toll
an Lochain
Loch Tuil
Bhearnach
Carn nan Gobhar
3255ft (992m)
Coire an t-Sith
GLENCANNICH FOREST
To Cannich
Mullach na Maole
2496ft (761m)
Allt Mullardoch
Mullardoch
House
Start
AST BENULA FOREST
Loch
a' Bhàna
Loch Sealbhanach
LOCH MULLARDOCH
Mullardoch Dam
Glen   Cannich
Creag a' Bhaca
FASNAKYLE FOREST
Coire Domhain
Allt a' Choire Dhomhain
Toll Creagach
3458ft (1054m)
To Cannich
Tom a' Chòinich
3645ft (1111m)
sh-
ch
b
re
nuill
Gleann   nam   Fiadh
Loch Beinn a' Mheadhoin
Glen   Affric
Loch Affric
iver Affric

Ah, Munros – how that name has changed attitudes and perceptions in the hill game over the past ten or so years. How that name has changed so many who would otherwise probably have never been seen dead in a pair of leather walking-boots and a woolly bob-hat! Munro-bagging is now not only respectable but trendy. It doesn't seem all that long ago that climbers referred to such people as dirty Munro-baggers. The prefix was always there, proclaimed with a sneer, a deliberate put-down, a reference to a lesser mortal. But now climbers and mountaineers themselves are in on the act, openly admitting to the fact that if the conditions are not good for climbing, then they might just go off and bag a Munro or six!

In recent years there has been an awareness of keeping fit and healthy. Look at the jogging boom of the 1970s, then the marathon-running boom. Walking, as a leisure activity, is now more popular than ever. Nineteen ninety-one, the centenary of the appearance of *Munro's Tables*, saw the publication of several guides to the Munros, including my own *The Munro Almanac*, which has since sold about 30 000 copies, and in the same year Muriel Gray broadcasted her television series *The Munro Show*. This, probably more than any other single programme, brought the beauty of the hills into sitting-rooms, and suddenly people realized that hill-walking wasn't only for pseudo-hardmen with beards and icicles dangling from their nostrils. They could do it too.

Most people like to have some form of framework on which to hang their odd passions, and the Munros offer such a hook. They also bring a methodology, a purpose to the rather aimless (but fine) occupation of stravaiging – just wandering – the hills.

This is the opposite of the way I began listing Munros. Like many of my contemporaries, I tramped the hills in summer and winter with never a thought of Munros. I was aware of Munros. I knew how many there were and where most of them were, but much of my hill time was taken up with other hill games – climbing rock in summer and snow and ice in winter, skiing, both downhill and touring, and cross-country skiing through the forests when conditions allowed.

It wasn't until I read Hamish Brown's book, *Hamish's Mountain Walk*, the story of climbing all the Munros in a single expedition, that I began to wonder how many I had climbed. I bought *Munro's Tables*, spent hours searching old diaries and my memory, and came up with a figure that approached 200. It took me another twelve years to climb the remainder, completing them on Ben More on Mull in 1991. On completion I decided to begin all over again, and in the five years since have climbed about 175 for the second time, and that was the reason I was wandering around the twelve Munros of Loch Mullardoch – I was ticking my list for the second time. To many people this may seem an odd thing to do, but in the course of climbing 277 mountains it's astonishing how many views you miss because of cloud or low visibility – a case of another view mist (sic)! It's also astonishing how many memories of the hills you take home with you, and wallow in the nostalgia as you visit them for the second, third or fourth time.

Loch Mullardoch Dam to Carn Eige

•

I had left my car beside the dam and immediately began the long climb up on to Toll Creagach. Even at the early hour the sun was hinting that the day would be a hot one and each tiny puddle and lochan gave off a shimmering mirage. It was good to sit by the cairn on the summit and contemplate both the view and the rest of the walk. Immediately beside me, Tom a' Chòinich looked fairly benevolent, but before I took to its long eastern ridge it would be time for lunch. I shouldered the pack again and dropped down to the bealach in search of water, a brew and a bite to eat.

Toll Creagach represents the start of a long undulating ridge which follows the south side of Loch Mullardoch for several miles, down to a broad bealach, over the rounded top of Tom a' Chòinich, then over several intermediary tops before another climb to the start of Carn Eige's eastern ridge. In three big mountain days I hoped to climb Toll Creagach (3458 feet/1054 m), Tom a' Chòinich (3645 feet/1111 m), Carn Eige (3881 feet/1183 m), Beinn Fhionnlaidh (3297 feet/1005 m), Màm Sodhail (3871 feet/1180 m), An Socach (3018 feet/920 m), Sgurr nan Ceathreamhnan (3776 feet/ 1151 m), Mullach na Dheiragain (3222 feet/982 m), An Socach (3507 feet/1069 m), An Riabhachan (3704 feet/1129 m), Sgurr na Lapaich (3773 feet/1150 m) and Carn nan Gobhar (3255 feet/992 m). I was carrying camping gear for two nights out – but the major problem was the heat. It was like walking uphill in an oven!

After the usual caffeine fix I tramped up the steep and rocky slope which leads to Tom a' Chòinich, coming across the end result of someone's breakfast, or it might have been dinner. Whatever it represented had come right through his or her system and sat slap-bang in the middle of the narrow pathway, topped with a little crown of white toilet paper. I couldn't believe it. It's hard to understand the base instinct that makes someone stop and squat right in the middle of a route where he must know others will follow.

Mass defecation in the hills is a burgeoning problem, and this was the worst example of man's intolerance of others I'd ever come across. No, one example was worse. It was when I was climbing a winter snow and ice route in Coire an t-Sneachda in the Cairngorms. I had spent over an hour tackling a long snowy groove which I knew led to a small ledge where I could tie myself on and belay my companion. Imagine my disgust as I pulled up on to the ledge to find it already occupied by a pile of excrement. If there is one thing worse than eyeballing a turd at close range it must be trying to kick it off the ledge while wearing crampons. Within seconds I had it all over the place.

It's interesting that at the same time as the Nepalese authorities announced plans to build a toilet block at Everest base camp, some local councillors in Fort William thought the time had come to build a toilet somewhere up the Ben Nevis tourist track.

ABOVE: THE EASTERN SUMMIT OF AN RIABHACHAN LIFTS ITS HEAD ABOVE THE CLOUDS.
THIS, 'THE BRINDLED, GREYISH ONE', IS A LONG RIDGE WHICH IS TIGHT AND EXPOSED IN PLACES.
LEFT: THE AUTHOR NEAR THE BEGINNING OF THE WALK ON THE SLOPES OF TOLL CREAGACH;
THE BLUE WATERS OF LOCH MULLARDOCH LIE BELOW.

•

Farmers on the Pennine Way, which runs up the backbone of northern England from Edale in Derbyshire to the Scottish Borders, have been complaining about the problem for years, and a gamekeeper of my acquaintance has been driven almost crazy by one of his best dogs which has a penchant for rolling in the stuff whenever it finds it – and such are the numbers of folks in hills that finding it is becoming increasingly easy.

The answer to the problem is a simple one. Everyone who goes to wild places should carry a small trowel with which to dig a cat-hole. The stuff, and the offending TP, should be buried. I don't claim to be the originator of this piece of wise counsel, but a quote from that great book of eternal wisdom, the Bible, says it all: 'Designate a place outside the camp where you can go to relieve yourself. As part of your equipment have something to dig with, and when you relieve yourself, dig a hole and cover up your excrement.' (Deuteronomy 23:12,13.) Simple, really!

From Tom a' Chòinich westwards the broad undulating ridge eases itself into slimmer proportions, as its flanks are eaten into by great corries. Cross the deep notch of the Garbh-bhealach and encounter the needles and pinnacles of Stob Coire Dhomhnuill, a classic scramble along the notched, prickly crest. It always amuses me that the various guidebooks suggest scrambles like this, with the corollary that a good footpath runs along the side! For lesser mortals, of course.

The path weaves its way nicely through the pinnacles and then climbs to another top, Stob a' Choire Dhomhain, from where the ridge broadens in a wide sweep all the way to the huge cairn on Carn Eige. Just north of here, sitting out on a broad one-mile limb, Beinn Fhionnlaidh sits in seclusion, mocking the ticker and collector of Munros. On my first round it took me three attempts to 'bag' this hill, and it was only a stroke of luck that allowed me to climb it the third time. Lack of time was my excuse when I first climbed Carn Eige and Màm Sodhail from Gleann nam Fiadh. It was winter, and we just couldn't afford the two hours to head out to Fhionnlaidh and back before darkness. The second time gale-force winds and torrential rain made me turn back on Tom a' Chòinich, and it was some time before I managed a third attempt. By this time I was tidying up all the odd Munros I hadn't climbed, and there at the top of the list was Beinn Fhionnlaidh. A friend and I took the familiar road by Cannich to Glen Affric, and only when we picked our rucksacks out of the car boot did we realize that neither of us had brought a map or a compass.

The morning was dour with thick cloud, but we decided to head up on to the Carn Eige ridge anyway, and as we climbed the low cloud seemed to lift with us. By the time we breasted the ridge the sky was clear and there was our Munro, less mocking than it had appeared hitherto. The day stayed good, and I got my hill.

This second visit to Beinn Fhionnlaidh ('Finlay's Hill') brought its own problems. Finding good drinking-water is rarely a problem in the Scottish hills, but it was today. All the way across to Fhionnlaidh and back, the streams were dry and I was developing a raging thirst. I had planned a high-level camp on the bealach between Eige and Màm

Sodhail, but a few hundred feet below the saddle the sun was hitting patches of silver – springs of water, reflecting like jewels, and at that moment just as precious. I dropped down to camp, literally!

Carn Eige to Coire Lungard

•

I awoke in the morning feeling hot and bothered. The sun had risen over the bealach behind me and was heating up the tent with the effect of a 500-watt sunray lamp. It was a morning for an alfresco breakfast. There's something magical about waking up high on a mountain. The obvious bonus is that you don't have to start the day with a huge climb, and twenty minutes after breaking camp I was on the summit of Màm Sodhail. It was obviously going to be another hot day, and I relished the prospect of a cool breeze on the ridge – but there wasn't any. On the plus side, however, the views were every bit as wide as they had been the day before, although, to begin with, many of the far western hills were hidden under a wrap of low cloud which would soon burn off in the hot sun.

The cairn on Màm Sodhail is the biggest one I've seen, a relic of an old Ordnance Survey station. This particular summit was used in a survey in the 1840s, and apparently the cairn once stood over twenty feet in height. Just below the summit, on the ridge leading down to the Bealach Coire Ghaidheil, lie the remains of a surveyor's shelter.

From Màm Sodhail the ridge to Sgurr nan Ceathreamhnan flows on in a long sweeping curve, but its undulations are gentle and all the broad bealachs are well peppered with pools and lochans. On a previous Munro trip I had backpacked in to Alltbeithe from the Clunie Inn and climbed An Socach, Sgurr nan Ceathreamhnan and Mullach na Dheiragain in the afternoon. It had been a cloudy day and only one aspect of the walk stands out in my memory – the long, long hike out to Mullach na Dheiragain from Ceathreamhnan. It makes Beinn Fhionnlaidh look like a mere afterthought.

The descent of Màm Sodhail can be tiring on bouldery, scree-covered ground. The secret is to deviate off the main ridge on to the north-west slopes, where a footpath works a way through the screes. I didn't, and stumbled my way down a steepish and incredibly loose ridge to the flat boggy Bealach Coire Ghaidheil. My efforts at keeping my feet had made me hot, and it was good to stand in a pool of water for a few minutes.

I must admit I felt just a bit foolish, ankle-deep in brown, bracken-filled water, as another walker came over the peat hag immediately in front of me. A man in his middle fifties, he looked to be moving slowly, but there was something about his gait which was methodical and rhythmic. I wasn't surprised when he told me he had come over the Lapaichs and Mullach na Dheiragain the day before and was returning to the

Mullardoch Dam, taking the route I had come that day. He was walking my three-day route in two in what was a quick and effective Munro-bagging raid.

The next summit, An Socach ('the snout'), must be a name that for some mysterious reason has offended the Ordnance Survey, for neither this hill nor its name-sake on the other side of Loch Mullardoch are named on the map. I suppose that the OS, unshackled from the odd rules of the Munro game, simply saw An Socach as yet another blip on the long ridge from Màm Sodhail to Ceathreamhnan, just as it probably saw the northern An Socach as a mere westward extension of An Riabhachan. Hills like these show up the anomalies of the Munros, in particular the fact that there has never been a strict guideline about what constitutes a 'top' from a separate mountain.

The Corbetts, the Scottish peaks of 2500–2999 feet, have a re-ascent of 500 feet on all sides, a clear definition, but it sometimes feels that the Munros lack such definition, clear rules or guidelines, and I like that. In a world that is becoming increasingly dominated by regulations and rules – and you only have to look at the Euro-bureaucracy to get a hint of the increasing chaos – it's refreshing to discover a game that is distinctly lacking in standard regulation. For at the end of the day what does it matter? There is no competition at stake, no laurel wreaths or five-figure cheques – the Munros just don't matter. Being out there is what counts, on the hills, enjoying the uplift, the beauty, the essence of the green world.

Sgurr nan Ceathreamhnan ('the peak of the quarters') has been described in the Scottish Mountaineering Club's guide to the Munros as 'one of the great prizes for the Scottish hill-walker'. (It seems it's hard to escape this notion that we're in competition with the hills – dammit, we're not!) This is a big and complex hill, as the name suggests, with at least four long sinewy ridges radiating out from a summit that forms the apex of five huge corries and the longest ridge of all running for over four miles to the head of Loch Mullardoch. Somewhere in about the middle of that ridge lay my last Munro of the day, Mullach na Dheiragain.

I seemed to take a long time to reach it, along a dry and undulating ridge, and I was hot and thirsty. My feet were well and truly fired up, as though I had a handful of gravel in my boots, and I was now looking forward to a camp. I forced myself not to think about tomorrow – if it looked like being hot again I could always just walk out along the footpath that runs along the northern shore of Loch Mullardoch. I didn't really care that much about climbing the Munros – or did I?

By the time I had descended to the head of Loch Mullardoch the sun had gone down considerably and it was cooler – but the midges were out. The only answer was to try to get a bit of height and hope for a faint breeze. So I skirted the heathery slopes of Meall Shuas and made my way slowly up beside the chattering waters of the Allt Coire Lungard. The upper corrie was a deer-infested place – they were so wiped out by the heat that they merely looked at me and shrugged – and a small flat of green grass made the perfect campsite. After a quick meal I slept the sleep of the dead.

ABOVE: DESCENDING FROM MÀM SODHAIL
TO AN SOCACH, THE VIEWS ACROSS THE HILLS OF
AFFRIC AND GLEN SHIEL SHOW WHY THIS AREA IS
FAST BECOMING ONE OF THE MOST POPULAR
HILLWALKING AREAS IN THE COUNTRY.

LEFT: LOCH MULLARDOCH FROM HIGH ON CARN
EIGE. A WONDERFUL ARRAY OF HILLS SURROUND
THIS LONG, LONELY INLAND LOCH.

•

Coire Lungard to Loch Mullardoch Dam

•

This was to be the highlight of the round, 10 miles (16 km) and some 6000 feet (1830 m) of climbing, but could I cope with it if the weather was as hot as it had been? The still of the morning had a calming effect, with low mists blanketing the corrie. I had a long climb, over 2000 feet (610 m), to the summit of An Socach, up to the head of the corrie and then a long pull over grassy slopes to the summit ridge. As I climbed in and out of thin swirling mists I was aware of an eeriness, a curious atmosphere, an awareness that something strange was happening around me. The thin melancholy whistle of golden plover was an accompaniment to the coughs of red deer hinds. They, the creatures of the high corries, seemed to be unsettled too.

Not until I breasted the summit ridge and looked eastwards did I realize what it was: the whole of Scotland was covered in a sea of cloud, with only the top 500–800 feet of the mountaintops jutting out – a classic temperature inversion. Behind me, Coire Lungard and the slopes I had just climbed were beginning to fill in with cloud as well. Above, the sky was a cloudless blue, and the sun, even at this early hour of seven o'clock, was hot. But with the sea of cloud dissipating some of the heat, romping along the ridge was a pure and unadulterated delight, high above this white and seemingly impenetrable world.

A short descent into the cloud-filled bealach was followed by a climb up on to the sweeping, curving ridge of An Riabhachan, 'the brindled, greyish one'. This ridge has two main parts: the north-west section, which is tight and exposed and connects the western top and the south-western top, and the main ridge, a long, broad and level affair which allows you to look ahead to the shapely Sgurr na Lapaich, one of the finest hills in the western Highlands. Such thoughts would have been far from the mind of a certain Mrs Waugh, who landed here in a helicopter a few years ago *en route* to the maternity hospital in Inverness from Skye. Her son Mark was born during a snowstorm on the summit of An Riabhachan – the youngest person ever to be on a Munro.

It's a big drop down to the bealach above Loch Mor, the Bealach Toll an Lochain, and I begrudged every foot of descent. I knew I had a climb of about 1200 feet (366 m) to the summit of Sgurr na Lapaich and had resolved to take it easy – slowly and steadily. The sun, high in the sky by now, was burning up the cloud at a tremendous rate and great gaps and rifts were appearing, like a curtain on fire. By the time I reached the summit of Sgurr na Lapaich all the cloud had gone, the sun once more reigned supreme, and the landscape seemed to be bracing itself for another onslaught of merciless heat.

A narrow and rocky rib forms the beginning of Sgurr na Lapaich's south-eastern ridge, and after clambering around on some soft, slobbery snow I took to a long gully which was still filled with snow. It was really too soft for glissading, but it did cool the feet and I wasn't long in reaching the foot of Carn nan Gobhar, the last top of the round. It was good to sit by the summit cairn and look back at the magnificent eastern aspect of Sgurr na Lapaich, its big, steep corries shimmering above the waters of Loch Tuil Bhearnach. Beyond the mountain lay the big hills of Loch Monar and Glen Carron; beyond those the elephantine tops of Torridon, unmistakable in outline. Some day-walkers passed by, commenting on the fact that the weather had improved since the cloud had gone. I wanted to tell them that high above them, above the glens and the houses and the roads, the weather had been perfect since dawn, but I didn't. It seemed unfair, so I picked up my pack, said goodbye to the Munros, and took to the long slopes of Carn nan Gobhar back to Loch Mullardoch, my car and that other world to which I also belong.

CHAPTER EIGHT

HARRIS

EXPLORING THE WILDERNESS ON THE LONG ISLE

•

Richard Else

A two- to three-day walk in the hills of North Harris

MAP: *OS 1:50 000 Sheet 13*
START: *Bunavoneadar, on the B887. Grid Ref: 132042*
FINISH: *Hushinish, on the B887. Grid Ref: 990120*
LENGTH: *20 miles (32 km)*
APPROXIMATE TIME: *2–3 days*
TERRAIN: *Rough walking, sometimes with no evident path but with no other difficulties*
ACCOMMODATION: *In Tarbert, the nearest town, there's the well-established hospitality of the Harris Hotel
and also an enterprising fish and chip shop*
TRANSPORT: *Ferries to Lewis and Harris sail from Ullapool to Stornoway and from Uig to Tarbert. The only bus
service runs between Stornoway and Tarbert, and times of buses need to be checked as they vary on
different days of the week*
SPECIAL NOTE: *Sunday is still strictly observed on Harris and Lewis – expect to find everywhere closed*

Tucked away in the introduction to the Scottish Mountaineering Club's 1934 guidebook *The Islands of Scotland* is a curious little acknowledgement. The editor, the legendary Scottish climber Naismith, is thanking his correspondent J. A. Parker for writing the chapter on the Outer Hebrides, which group of islands 'he has visited no less than four times'. Such a sentiment aptly reminds us of how isolated the islands of Barra, Uist, Benbecula and Lewis and Harris were a mere half-century ago and how easy, comparatively speaking, travel is today. The newly commissioned ferry from Ullapool to Stornoway has shrunken the time from the four hours on my first visit to just two and a half hours, while the journey from Uig, on Skye's north-western tip, to Tarbert on Harris is only 105 minutes.

Yet travel times have done little to diminish the splendour of the largest of these islands – Harris and Lewis. Although always referred to as two separate islands, they are in fact one piece of land and the largest island in the Outer Hebrides. I remember

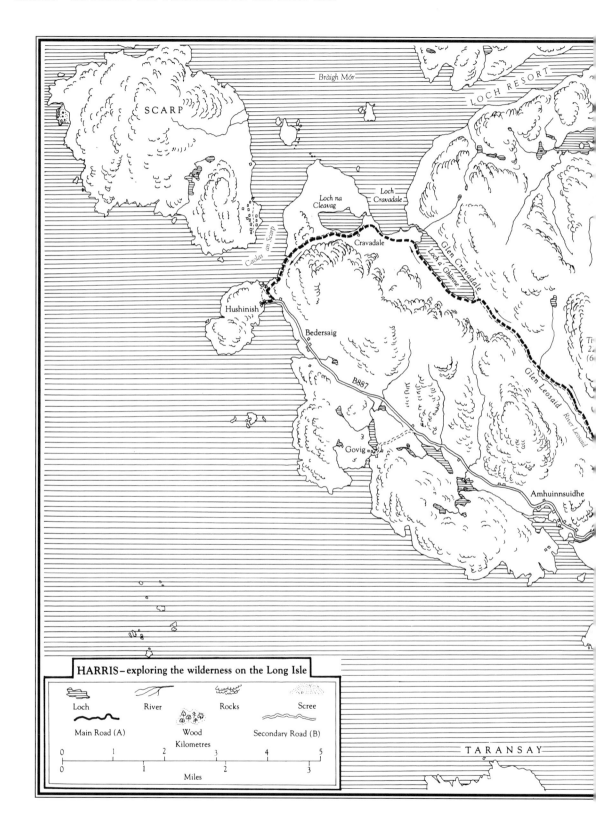

Bràigh Mór

LOCH RESORT

SCARP

Loch na
Cleavag

Loch
Cravadale

Cravadale

Glen Cravadale

Loch a' Ghlinne

Caolas an Scarp

Hushinish

Bedersaig

B887

Glen Leosaid

River Leosaid

Govig

Amhuinnsuidhe

HARRIS – exploring the wilderness on the Long Isle

Loch   River   Rocks   Scree

Main Road (A)   Wood   Secondary Road (B)

Kilometres

0   1   2   3   4   5

0   1   2   3

Miles

TARANSAY

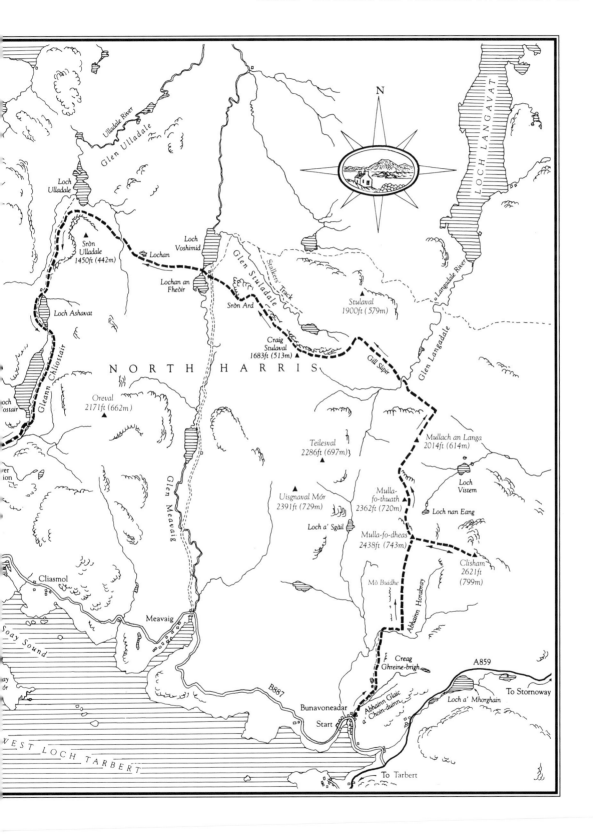

arriving for the first time over twenty years ago and discovering that Harris and Lewis are both literally and culturally a place apart from the mainland. Here, for example, Gaelic, which amazingly has no legal status as an official language, is the principal form of communication. Here the landscape, while being exceptionally attractive in many places, does not conform to traditional notions of beauty. Most important, perhaps, the communities that live here have maintained a culture that is unlike anywhere else in the UK, and, to take the most obvious example, the Sabbath is still strictly and universally observed. On my first visit I also made two other discoveries: I witnessed the ferocity of the storms that can quickly attack even in summer, rendering all progress exceptionally slow and painful. Secondly, I found a quiet but real warmth among many of the people I met, and that affection is what brought me back in the succeeding years.

There is also something very special about walking in both Harris and Lewis, and, although the mountains are not high when compared with the rest of Scotland, there is a real sense of wilderness that comes not only from being isolated from the rest of Britain but also from the paucity of the population. Lewis, for example, had a population of 20 159 at the last census in 1991, but over 8000 of these inhabitants live in or around the only significant town in the Western Isles – Stornoway. The population of Harris was just over 2000. Yet half a century ago it was more than double that, at nearly 5000. Like so many rural communities, the lack of paid employment has resulted in significant depopulation and a complex web of problems that one writer has described as 'intractable'. The visitor to Harris sees one of the most intriguing landscapes in Britain, but like so many other wilderness areas it is to a greater or lesser extent man-made. At the time of writing a fierce debate is raging about the proposed 'super-quarry' on South Harris; and while many walkers and conservationists feel that this would ruin a valuable part of the island, one local man put another side of the argument forcibly to me. 'Would you like it,' he said, 'if everybody told you your business and said they know best? We have to live too, and a job's a job.'

It was with this sense of both the romantic and the practical that Sara, who was waiting patiently for the results of her GCSEs, and I arrived at the small port of Tarbert one Friday morning with a plan to explore the mountains to the north of the village. It was her first visit to the Outer Hebrides, and we had chosen a three-day walk of approximately twenty miles which would illustrate a wide variety of scenery, from mountaintops, through deep glens that punctuate the landscape like long fingers, to the twisting coastline with its machair (distinctive low grassy land). This walk can be undertaken without your own transport, although it is useful for exploring the remainder of the island which has many places of historical interest, not least the standing stones at Callanish.

After disembarking at Tarbert, we headed north for two miles on the A859 before taking the road west for approximately another twelve or so. In fact, you simply travel along the northern side of West Loch Tarbert, zigzagging to and fro until the road ends at Hushinish. We decided to leave our car here, at what is, in fact, the end of the walk, and then took a taxi to the beginning of it. A word of warning is in order here: both the OS 1:50 000 and 1:25 000 maps show telephone boxes at Hushinish and near Meavaig; in fact, these no longer exist – although there is one, unmarked on the maps, next to the post office just west of Amhuinnsuidhe (reference 043083). More by good luck than judgement we had arranged our taxi before leaving Tarbert and were collected by John Norman McKinnon. He's a native of Harris, and as we headed back along the road for our starting-point of Bunavoneadar we chatted about the challenges faced by all rural areas and of the frequent need people have to do a variety of jobs in order to make ends meet. We also spoke about the importance of Gaelic and how some of John Norman's children, now adults, had managed to use it in their jobs. We could have chatted the afternoon away, but before parting I asked if he had ever climbed Clisham, which was our immediate objective, and John Norman said no, but that he had enjoyed looking at it and that was enough!

Bunavoneadar to Mullach an Langa

•

As we left the tiny settlement at Bunavoneadar, we followed a path leading steadily upwards by the Abhainn Glaic a' Choin-duinn (unnamed on the 1:50 000 map) but stopped to look back at the remains of the old whaling-station and its prominent chimney. This is all that remains of what was once the heart of a Western Isles whaling industry. Until 1922 the station had been operated by a Norwegian company, but in that year it was purchased by Lord Leverhulme as part of his plan for the economic regeneration of the island. Leverhulme's ambitious schemes for both Lewis and Harris make fascinating, sombre, complicated reading, and it is ironic that his aspirations for the whaling-station failed because of lack of demand for whale products.

Seen from the south, both Mulla-fo-dheas and Clisham present a fine, rounded shape and are formed of Lewisian gneiss – one of the oldest rocks in the world. The way ahead is clear and begins by contouring under the face of Creag Ghreine-brigh before making a rising traverse of the Abhainn Horabray. Then a line directly north is followed, first to the promontory of Mò Buidhe and onwards to Mulla-fo-dheas at 2438 feet (743 m). At first the walking is through tussocky grass, then, as you head up Mò Buidhe, it is across boulders and loose stones. This landscape is a primitive one: almost as if the work of creation is not yet finished. In summer it was hard, hot work, with Sara and I treating ourselves to a number of regular breaks, ostensibly for us to look at the view, but in reality for us to get our breath back. The view southwards across West Loch Tarbert is not to be underestimated, and despite the heat-haze we could see far into the south-western corner of the island. After the toil up to the summit, we could look both northwards along this fine, long ridge to the final high point of Mullach an Langa and eastwards to Clisham. At 2621 feet (799 m), Clisham is the highest mountain on Harris – in fact the only one over 2460 feet (750 m) – and can be reached by a diversion to the east which takes you along a sharp ridge straight to its summit.

Explorers of these hills in the north of Harris will be struck by a splendour that is out of all proportion to the height. Sara had been talking about the isolation you feel when walking here, a sense of being the only people in an immense landscape; like me, she felt that these hills in the deer and treeless Forest of Harris were a true mountain environment. Walking there also reinforced my dislike of Munro-bagging and the opinion that height alone is important. I have heard it said that Munro-bagging is a harmless pursuit and a good way for people to get to know a large part of Scotland, but I am unconvinced by that argument and I think that mountains should not be judged by their height alone. Let it just be said that these mountains of Harris have their own special aura, and their situation is what makes them particularly special.

Mulla-fo-dheas is at the heart of a long ridge that curves round to Clisham. We were now heading north to its other extremity, and we began by descending a short, narrow section (which is not as intimidating as it looks) before heading upwards again to the slightly lower point of Mulla-fo-thuath at 2362 feet (720 m). Incidentally, because of the island's history, pure Gaelic names are rare on the hills; many of them are Norse or a hybrid of Gaelic and Norse. However, these two summits are 'pure' Gaelic with Mulla-fo-thuath meaning 'north summit' and Mulla-fo-dheas 'south summit'. Given the rich descriptions of many Gaelic names, I was somewhat disappointed by these translations until I learnt, with some surprise, that such direct geographical references are unusual.

Like all good ridge walks, this one entices you onwards until you stand on the top of its final peak, Mullach an Langa. On the mile or so of the ridge you get excellent close-up views of the crags on the eastern side of Mulla-fo-dheas followed by the shattered rock faces that form the western side of Mulla-fo-thuath, and an airy sense of being high above Loch a' Sgàil. Although we had now descended a little way, to 2014 feet (614 m), standing on the top of Mullach an Langa gave another excellent vantage point. It was now early evening, and to the south-east there was the prominent pointed top of Clisham with the final hundred yards or so glowing pink in the setting sun. Away northwards, in a panorama of water and earth, was the finger of Loch Langavat curling north-eastwards, with the glint of numerous smaller lochans, and to the west was the rounded bulk of the landscape we would be travelling over in the next few days. Although water was scarce on the higher ground, we descended on the eastern

ABOVE: UISGNAVAL MÓR AND CLISHAM
ACROSS WEST LOCH TARBERT.
THE HILLS OF HARRIS ARE IN STARK
CONTRAST TO THE FLAT PEATY MOORS OF
LEWIS, THE NORTHERN PART OF THE
LONG ISLE.

RIGHT: EVENING LIGHT ON THE HIGH
TOPS OF HARRIS. UISGNAVAL MÓR AND
UISGNAVAL BEAG WITH CLISHAM
BEYOND, FROM ULLAVAL.

side of the cliff face that guards Mullach an Langa and camped just below the 400-metre contour line. Our reward, in addition to an absence of midges that inhabit this part of Harris, was to look at a landscape that seemed utterly unchanged through the passing of centuries and where, to the best of our knowledge, we appeared to be the only people. Our dome tent and few possessions seemed the merest pinprick on this scene. There was only the subdued roar from our stove as we made drinks and a late meal while we watched the moon rise over this primitive landscape.

Glen Langadale to Glen Leosaid
•

Next morning we headed down to Glen Langadale, taking care underfoot on the rocky, tussocky ground. As we headed up the opposite side by the delightful Gill Slipir, we stopped for a drink alongside some well-preserved shielings (marked only on the 1:25 000 map) and wondered exactly who their occupants had been, what lives they had led and how they viewed this vast, wild landscape. Higher up, we picked up the stalkers' path that starts by Langadale River and leads to the coll at 1161 feet (354 m). Sara and I had planned our route at some length, aware that an infinite variety of ways can be taken across this wild country. In the end we had chosen a line to show the variety of scenery and to give an insight into the sombre beauty and grandeur of this special island. We were also aware that in most conditions walking through this wilderness is far harder than the altitude or actual distance would suggest. Away from the coast, much of the walking at lower levels is over boggy, rough ground of tufted heather, and across boulder-strewn slopes higher up. We now made our way south-west to Craig Stulaval (1683 feet/513 m) which gave superb views, including Stulaval (slightly higher at 1900 feet/579 m) to the north-east, Teilesval in the south, and the distinctive shape of deer breaking the skyline further around to the west. As we wandered lazily along the summit plateau towards Sròn Ard, we were fascinated by the cliff faces plunging down into Glen Stuladale and peered down almost a thousand feet to see the distinct snake of the stalkers' track making its way to the head of the glen. In the diffuse light the rocks nearby were magically illuminated, while in the distance everything was an ethereal blur lost in shades of green, blue and grey.

It was on our descent from Sròn Ard that we had our first contact with another person. A walker out for the day was making his rapid way up Glen Meavaig, but he had passed northwards well before we arrived at the track. Crossing between Loch Voshimid and Lochan an Fheòir was easily accomplished by stepping-stones, but the sheer tranquillity of the scene seemed a good enough reason to stop for lunch.

A parked four-wheel-drive vehicle suggested that fishermen were hereabouts, but we ate in peace and quiet accompanied only by the murmur of water running from the smaller to the larger loch. In a landscape where even a century is just a passing moment, we were witnessing a scene that had little changed for possibly thousands of years. Had it been cooler we would have stayed longer, but a combination of the heat and the realization that we had a good distance still to travel compelled us to finish one last drink and move on. Sharing experiences you enjoy with your children is not always easy, but looking at Sara's face and her determined stride even with a full pack made me realize that she too shared in my feeling that this wilderness is quite unlike any other in Scotland.

Afterwards we headed further west, and although only about 500 feet of ascent it was a hard slog up to the lochan at 709 feet (216 m). We then followed an indistinct track where the descent was almost as hard as the pull up to arrive at Loch Ulladale. Here a gillie and his client were trying their luck, their boat sweeping back and forth across the loch. Yet attractive as this loch undoubtedly is, the scene is dominated by the towering, overhanging form of Sròn Ulladale. Passing underneath this huge mass of rock reveals its many different facets, including some fearsome overhanging sections, as you contour around from the north-eastern face to the western one. It towers over 800 feet above the loch and provides a number of challenging routes for climbers. The first recorded route dates back to 1938, but in recent years some of the best climbers in Britain have been enticed here; looking up at the many lines on the rock, it is not hard to see why.

We now turned south down Glen Ulladale, following the well-defined path, and were grateful for its well-constructed gradients as we ascended almost 650 feet to the head of the glen and the high-level Loch Ashavat. This loch marks the watershed between Glen Ulladale and Gleann Chliostair. Its waters flow not north but south into the larger Loch Chliostair – which is actually a reservoir. Its shore offers good views west to Tirga Mór and south down the Gleann to the head of the loch. After the hard work earlier in the day, it was a relief to wander along this path knowing that our progress was quick and without the pain of previous exertions. As our feet seemed to move without any conscious thought, I reflected on the day's walking. While it was still a delight to be making such effortless movement, I missed the sense of exploration we'd felt earlier when Sara and I had being following less trodden ways. I wondered about visitors who had walked here just a hundred years ago, when maps were less accurate and local knowledge would have been even more vital. Theirs must have been a real exploration.

After Loch Chliostair the path widens into a private road, with a pipeline from the reservoir alongside right the way down to a small hydroelectric power-station. This insignificant-looking building generates almost all the electricity needed on Harris and must be an incredible model of efficiency – by comparison with the huge power-stations found in industrial areas, this looks more like a large garden shed.

Above: Beautiful Hebridean light on Loch na Cleavag and Loch Cravadale, Hushinish.

Far Left: The view to Loch Voshimid.

Left: Part of the attraction of wilderness walking is the fact that you have to carry everything you need in a pack on your back. Modern lightweight tents make fine mobile home-from-homes.

•

Glen Cravadale to Hushinish

•

Turning westwards from Glen Leosaid is another ruined settlement and plenty of opportunities for camping, although in summer the midges can be a problem almost anywhere. Once the journey down Glen Cravadale and by Loch a' Ghlinne is underway, this walk changes character from inland to coastal, with heather giving way to machair. There are superb views away northwards where the landscape and seascape are inextricably intertwined. The situation of Cravadale, a solitary cottage by Loch na Cleavag, must be one of the best in Britain. Today it isn't permanently occupied, and a prominent 'H' nearby suggests that the owner has a quick form of transport to get here!

Finally, the coast path leads back to the tiny crofting community of Hushinish, and we placed our rucksacks by the side of the Land Rover and watched the waves break across the emptiness of the bay, remembering that while people have inhabited these islands for perhaps 6000 years their impact upon this wild landscape is still insignificant. Which is remarkable when you think that this island was probably first settled by a Mediterranean people in the Stone or Bronze Age and then by a succession of incomers, including Picts, Scandinavians and Celts.

Sara and I had spoken about many things on our walk but her impending GCSE results had somehow been forgotten. It was time to drive back to Tarbert and to the hospitality of the Harris Hotel. There we enjoyed a well-earned celebration to a memorable few days. Which is what always happens when you come to somewhere as precious as this.

CHAPTER NINE

RATHAD NAM MEIRLEACH

THE THIEVES' ROAD

•

Cameron McNeish

Part 1: a two-day walk from Glenmore to Dalwhinnie via Rothiemurchus and Glen Feshie

---

MAPS: *OS 1:50 000 Sheets 35, 36 and 42*

START: *Pass of Ryvoan. Grid Ref: 002108*

FINISH: *Dalwhinnie, on the A9 Perth–Inverness road. Grid Ref: 634849*

LENGTH: *36 miles (58 km)*

APPROXIMATE TIME: *2 days*

TERRAIN: *Easy walking on footpaths*

ACCOMMODATION: *Loch Morlich has a youth hostel and Glenmore has some b&bs. The large Forestry Commission campsite at Glenmore has a regular bus service to and from Aviemore. There is also a bunkhouse, b&b and hotel accommodation in Dalwhinnie with a good tea-shop. Dalwhinnie is also on the London–Inverness railway*

It was a writer by the name of Colin Fletcher, a Welshman now domiciled in California, who coined a cardinal rule of travel which I believe is pertinent to everyone who goes walking. He calls it 'the law of inverse appreciation' and it came to mind as I watched a TV programme about a motor cyclist claiming that driving his big, high-powered bike brought him closer to the land. 'Hogwash,' I thought, or words to that effect.

Fletcher claims you can come close to the land only by walking on it – the less there is between you and the environment, the more you appreciate that environment, and I agree wholeheartedly. Most walkers know that the bigger and most efficient (which usually means oil guzzling and environmentally damaging) your means of travel, the further you become divorced from the reality through which you are travelling.

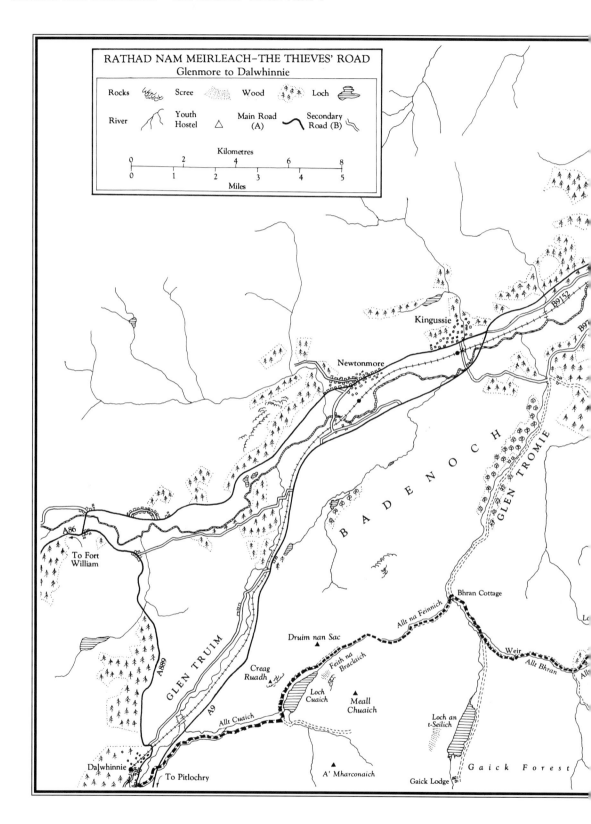

RATHAD NAM MEIRLEACH–THE THIEVES' ROAD
Glenmore to Dalwhinnie

Rocks   Scree   Wood   Loch

River   Youth   Main Road   Secondary
        Hostel   (A)   Road (B)

Kilometres
0   2   4   6   8
0   1   2   3   4   5
Miles

Kingussie

Newtonmore

BADENOCH

GLEN TROMIE

A86

To Fort
William

GLEN TRUIM

A889

A9

Druim nan Sac

Bhran Cottage

Allt na Feinnich

Weir

Allt Bhran

Creag
Ruadh

Feith na
Braclaich

Loch
Cuaich

Meall
Chuaich

Loch an
t-Seilich

Allt Cuaich

Gaick Forest

Dalwhinnie

To Pitlochry

A' Mharconaich

Gaick Lodge

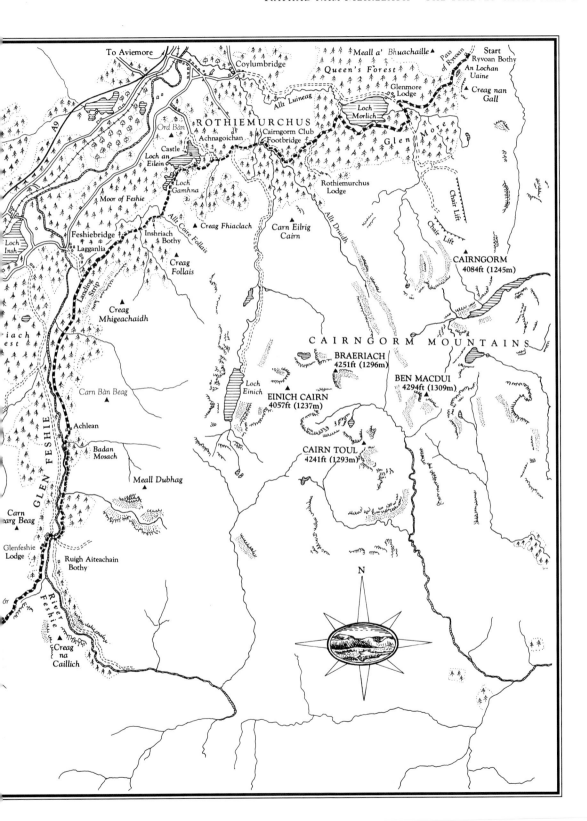

It's obvious that a solo yachtsman learns more about the sea than a passenger on the *QE2*!

Likewise, while you certainly remain closer in touch with the heartbeat of the land on a motor bike than you would in a super-luxury, air-conditioned motor coach, you come as close as you possibly can while on foot.

But Fletcher's law has a second and less obvious application: your appreciation varies not only according to what you travel in but also according to what you travel over. Drive along a motorway in any kind of car and the closest you come to tuning in to the landscape is the tune you hear from your car radio. Contact with the land you are travelling through is zero; you might as well be watching a television screen as the countryside whizzes past at seventy miles an hour. But turn off the motorway on to a country road, open the car window, and you come a tad closer. A narrow country road is better still, and a drive over flat grassland even better. However, you then step over the boundary of what is environmentally acceptable.

It's then that you discover a corollary to Fletcher's law: the further you move away from any impediment of appreciation, the better it is. By walking on a footpath you begin to appreciate the detail that turns a pretty countryside into a living, vibrant landscape. You bring other senses into play; you can smell the scent of warm sun on the pine resin, you can hear the cry of the skylark and the breath of the wind through the grasses.

That, according to Colin Fletcher, is being in touch with the world. Following in the footsteps of history also brings you closer to the land, to the whiffs and taints of things and people long since gone. The Pass of Ryvoan is both the beginning and the end of such an old trail, the end of a stealthy march by Lochaber clansmen in days long ago, a furtive journey through the quiet backwaters of the old district of Badenoch, a journey that took them through this pass towards the rich pastures – and rich takings – of Morayshire. Ryvoan was also the start of the return trip home, a more hazardous journey, driving the stolen cattle back along the same route, anxious to put as many miles between them and the plundered lands of Moray before daylight. Interestingly, this was a time when many of the western clans believed they had a divine right to lift the booty of the fertile Laich of Moray, an attitude summed up in a letter sent by Allan Cameron of Lochiel in 1645 to the Laird of Grant. In the letter, Lochiel apologizes most profusely for injuries inflicted on one of the Grants by some Cameron free-booters, explaining that the reivers had not known that the poor victim was a Grant but thought that he was a Morayman. Later in the letter, Lochiel recorded that the raid was intended to be 'to Morrayland, quhair all men taks their prey'.

This ancient route was known as Rathad nam Meirleach, 'the caterans' road' ('thieves' or robbers' road'), and not only was it the most direct route from Lochaber through Badenoch to Morayshire but it avoided the populous croftships and villages of Speyside, where the Lochaber men would no doubt have been resisted severely. Today the route is a logical one for backpackers who, for their own personal reasons, want to avoid the same places. My reasons were simple: I wanted to test Fletcher's law, to break free and read the small print of the land.

That wouldn't have been so simple for the caterans of old. From the pass, they would have crossed the Braes of Abernethy, probably at night, and rounded up the cattle of Dorback, Tomintoul and the surrounding districts, arriving back at Ryvoan with their grunting, sweating booty.

Ryvoan to Glen Feshie

•

The pass itself, between Creag Loisgte and Creag nan Gall, contrasts richly with the bare purple moors of Abernethy and Ryvoan. Below the scree-girt heights, pines, larches, birches and juniper grow in luxuriant profusion on a valley floor lush in green bracken, bilberry, cowberry and heather. This is a place long associated with the Little People. Here, at moonglow, fairies are said to come quietly and wash their emerald green clothing in the waters of An Lochan Uaine, a deep pool of aquamarine translucence surrounded by rocks and gnarled Scots pines. And it was hereabouts that Robin Oig, a Glenmore hunter, once came upon a green-clad fairy playing a tiny set of bagpipes. Robin snatched the pipes, and threw down his bonnet in exchange, only to see the pipes vanish into thin air, leaving in his hand a dead puffball to which three blades of grass were attached.

The Rathad nam Meirleach follows the Cairngorm ski road for a quarter of a mile and then escapes into Queen's Forest on a track that runs adjacent to the southern shore of Loch Morlich. The forest track winds on, now and then rising high above the gently lapping waters of the loch, the morning mists shimmering gently and slowly lifting as though the whole loch was exhaling in the early-morning air. Loch Morlich is a geological 'kettle hole', simply a great hole surrounded by glacial drift, and its outlet, the Allt Luineag, carving a slot westwards through the glacial debris and moraines. This geological description is an unfeeling one, for Loch Morlich is a fine stretch of water, fringed by golden beaches and backed by a solid wall of 4000-foot (1219-m) mountain, whose long-lying snow slopes, in winter and spring, contrast vividly with its dark green skirt of forest below.

This forest provides considerable shelter for wildlife during the inhospitable conditions that prevail for much of the year. Several roe-deer bounded across the track in front of me, ethereal in the still-evaporating morning mists, their coats a bright brownish red. A young solitary doe browsed at the edge of the forest. I stopped and froze, and slowly reached for my camera, which was hanging from my rucksack strap.

ABOVE: THE NORTHERN CORRIES OF THE CAIRNGORMS AND CARN EILRIG FROM LOCH MORLICH.
THE ROUTE OF THE THIEVES' ROAD FOLLOWS THE FAR SHORE OF THE LOCH AND THEN RUNS WESTWARDS
THROUGH THE ANCIENT CALEDONIAN PINES OF ROTHIEMURCHUS FOREST.

FAR LEFT: THE CALEDONIAN PINE FOREST PROVIDES CONSIDERABLE SHELTER FOR WILDLIFE DURING
THE NORMALLY INHOSPITABLE CONDITIONS WHICH PREVAIL FOR MUCH OF THE YEAR.

LEFT: SCOTS PINE CONES IN ROTHIEMURCHUS, THE FOREST OF TOMORROW.

Just as I managed to focus on her, she looked up at me, warned by some ancient instinct, and in the brief moment that her dark liquid eyes met mine through the lens of the camera, I was totally and utterly bewitched.

Her black nose twitched slightly, contrasting with the white wax-smooth pelage. Her eyes were dark and impenetrable, showing no sign of the fear that her instincts so surely must have been signalling to her, and as quickly as she looked up at me she was gone, vanished in a blur of precision and perfect deportment. I was left with an overwhelming wonder of the immensity of that moment as I gazed eye to eye into the beautiful world of nature. At that moment a barrier was removed, broken, and I stepped from one world into what Colin Fletcher refers to as 'the green world'. Sometimes that crossover takes a few days; at other times, like this, it takes only a few hours.

For the rest of that day the magnificent surroundings served only to exaggerate the new bond that had been formed between me and this natural world. In celebration, the track now meandered through a natural lavishness of Scots pine, birch and juniper, growing from a thick undergrowth ungrazed by either sheep or deer. It is a landscape little altered since the days when much of Scotland lay under the great mattress of the ancient Caledonian pine forest, that immensity of Scots pine which once stretched from coast to coast.

The prime relic is here at Rothiemurchus, a living museum of yesteryear. Blaeberries abound, ripe and luscious in July, and I passed carpets rich in cowberry, or cranberry, their white bell-like flowers and shiny evergreen leaves only just losing their bloom. I loafed along below the massive canopy of trees, each anchored deep in the peaty soil. They have trunks like the foremast of a sailing-ship, golden red, a colour perfectly offset by the bottle green effect of the foliage. In the streets of the mountains they have about them the quality of a bugle blast, and they are tenanted by pine marten, crossbills, crested tit and capercaillie, the horse-bird of the woods.

What happened to that ginormous forest? We have to go back 3000–4000 years to a race of people who were no wandering predators or scavengers. The Picts, or proto-Picts, were a polyandrous, matriarchal series of societies who were constantly preoccupied with looking for or creating clearings among the fearful forests that harboured wolves, bears and bandits. The young sons were obliged to move further and further away from their parents' holdings, to shielings that were progressively enlarged by the use of the axe and fire.

Later, Northmen, or Norsemen, burnt their way into the interior during their wild forays, and the process has been repeated over the centuries, reaching a climax with the terrible evictions in the early part of the nineteenth century when, to make grazing grounds for sheep, countless thousands of Scots pine were incinerated by the firesticks of the flockmasters. Rothiemurchus represents a noble example of what we have been left. We can now only dream of its former glory.

The morning mists had long since dissipated, and the sun now shone hot from a clear sky. The scent of pine resin drifted heavy in the air, and it was refreshing to leave the forest behind for the cooler moorland which stretches westwards to the forest that surrounds Loch an Eilein. This moorland was once forested too, but constant fellings during the two wars have left it as it is today. Like the southern shore of Loch Morlich, the track which twists around the southern shore of Loch an Eilein is also part of the original caterans' road. This loch is one of the most scenic in the Highlands. Completely surrounded by natural pine woods, it is an ornithologist's paradise, and even in the brief hour or so that I walked along its southern shore I saw siskins, wrens, chaffinches, crested tits, blue and coal tits, wagtails and, across the loch, spiralling high above the summit of Ord Bàn, a buzzard.

Over the waters, near the northern shore, lies the island that lends the loch its name, proudly bearing the last remains of its castle. Dating from the days of Robert the Bruce, Loch an Eilein Castle has been used by Comyns, Shaws and Grants, and legend has it that the infamous Wolf of Badenoch, one Alexander Stewart, the bastard son of Robert II of Scotland, once had a lair on the island stronghold.

At the south-western corner of the loch, a smaller stretch of water tags on almost as an afterthought. Loch Gamhna is a typical shallow reedy loch of the glaciated plain type. Backed by the rocky crags and pines of Kennapole Hill, known locally as the Cat's Den, Loch Gamhna has a tranquillity which Loch an Eilein and Loch Morlich lack. There are usually fewer people here too, despite the fact that a good track runs around the edge of the loch. As I walked along the path I flushed out a goosander and glimpsed the occasional mallard and teal as they hid themselves in the abundant reeds fringing the edges.

As the path straggles away from the shore, fording the shallow waters of the Allt Coire Follais which flows down between the pine-covered slopes of Creag Follais and Creag Fhiaclach, the highest natural tree-line you will find anywhere in Britain, you enter the stillness of yet another ancient forest – Inshriach. I soon came across a clearing that houses the small wooden cabin of Inshriach Bothy, a beautiful glade among the ancient pines, birches and dense juniper. Lorded over by a magnificent rowan tree, it was the perfect place for a mid-afternoon snack, the coolness sweet with the heady fragrance of bog myrtle and pine. As I ate, dragonflies whirred around me and chaffinches darted about by my feet, willing some crumbs to fall their way. It was a sore temptation to stop here for the night, pitching my tent on the luxurious grass which carpets the clearing, but I had an equally enchanting place in mind for the night's camp.

On I went over the winding track, past the dried-up silt and reeds of Lochan Gorm to the very edge of the Forestry plantation of Inshriach. Here, a crude, bulldozed track offends the senses as it runs westwards parallel to the Forestry fence. After a few hundred yards, another track leaves the boulders and rubble, crosses a small stream by way of a bridge, and then over a wide flood-plain to the south. On the western bank of the stream, a gate in the deer fence opens on to a Forestry road which leads to Glen Feshie.

A four-mile stretch of tarmac is usually endured rather than enjoyed, but this one carried me quickly to the farm at Achlean, where I skipped across to the riverside and followed a sketchy path alongside the fast-flowing River Feshie, through another forest plantation, and into the green magnificence of the upper glen near the old bothy of Ruigh Aiteachain.

This was my stop for the night, the paradise I had promised myself, rich in birdsong and wildlife, and luxuriant in lush vegetation. The more varied and profuse the vegetation, the richer is the birdlife, and so it is in Glen Feshie. Oystercatchers, sandpipers and curlews haunt the shingly riverbank, and meadow pipits, wheatears,

Top: Loch an Eilein is generally considered to be one of the loveliest lochs in Scotland. Surrounded by dense forest, it is bound on its southern shore by the long heather-covered slopes of the Sgurans ridge.

Left: The Cairngorms and the prominent defile of the Lairig Ghru rise solidly above the extensive Rothiemurchus Forest.

Right: The Kincardine Hills and Meall a' Bhuachaille rise above the hoar-frosted pines of the Queen's Forest in Glenmore, close to the start of the route.

•

larks and chats are common enough in the wild extravagance of juniper and birch. Red deer browse by the river and wander at ease through the woods of Scots pine. At the head of the riverflats in the south of the glen, Creag na Caillich ('the hill of the old woman'), stands sentinel, dividing the upper glen in two.

Glen Feshie to Dalwhinnie

•

The caterans' road leaves Feshie westwards before the Caillich is reached, and I followed its course in the company of a small herd of deer hinds, up a steep winding path, past a small brooding lochan, Lochan an t'Stuic, and on to the open moorland above. A small forest plantation blocked the way westwards, through which a faint path traces its way, avoiding the longer walk around its outskirts.

Southwards, the great rolling hills of Gaick stretched away into the distance below an even wider cloud-tumbled sky – typical Grampian scenery. I flushed out several red grouse, which burst from the heather in characteristic flight, their guttural 'go back, go back' taking me by surprise.

A footpath runs alongside the Allt Bhran, past a weir and down into the birch trees that grow beside the river in Glen Tromie. Further up the glen, past the old Bhran Cottage, a small bridge crosses the river, and an old stalkers' path runs for a short distance south-westwards beside the Allt na Feinnich. Across the boggy watershed I went, down to Loch Cuaich, nestling snugly below the steep craggy slopes of Meall Chuaich. As I followed a stream I noticed it was running the wrong way. Only then did I realize I had just crossed the watershed that runs up the spine of Scotland, the historic Druim Alban. On this occasion I planned to continue my journey right through to Fort William, and the remainder of the walk was now psychologically downhill.

To the south-west of me, across the busy A9, lay the long silver band of Loch Ericht, biting for some fifteen miles into the heart of Rannoch Moor. Although I was combining this walk with the next one, this would be the only road I would have to cross in the whole of the eighty miles from Glenmore to Fort William. It was still a good four miles off, so I didn't linger by Loch Cuaich. An aqueduct runs from the loch to Dalwhinnie, part of an intricate hydroelectric system of dams, power-stations and tunnels. A plaque at the end of Loch Cuaich pronounces: 'Cuaich–Seilich Tunnel, 22,310 feet, completed 1940.' Loch an t-Seilich lies in Gaick, where the waters from those high hills flow through this underground tunnel to Cuaich, down the aqueduct to Dalwhinnie and Loch Ericht, which has a dam at both ends, and from Ericht's south-western end drains to Rannoch Moor, which in turn feeds the Tummel–Pitlochry systems.

And I thought these hills allowed me to escape from twentieth-century technology!

CHAPTER TEN

RATHAD NAM MEIRLEACH

THE THIEVES' ROAD

•

Cameron McNeish

Part 2: a two-day walk from Dalwhinnie to Fort William

MAPS: *OS 1:50 000 Sheets 41 and 43*

START: *Dalwhinnie, on the A9 Perth–Inverness road. Grid Ref: 634849*

FINISH: *Fort William. Grid Ref: 113744*

LENGTH: *40 miles (64 km)*

APPROXIMATE TIME: *2–3 days*

TERRAIN: *Straightforward walking on footpaths*

ACCOMMODATION: *Dalwhinnie has a bunkhouse and hotel and b&b accommodation. There's a youth hostel at the western end of Loch Ossian and in Glen Nevis, and a private bunkhouse at the railway station at Corrour. Fort William has a wide range of accommodation to suit every taste and pocket, plus a good range of eating-places, including Indian and Chinese. The Crannog, a sea-food restaurant on Loch Linnhe, is superb, and you'll get a good lunch or snack in Nevisport*

Dalwhinnie, the highest village in the Scottish Highlands, may be a bleak and desolate corner of Badenoch, the sort of village where you half expect to see an antlered moose lumber across the road in front of you, but this *Northern Exposure* perception is softened by a good tea-room, a first-rate shop, a distillery and a railway station. A bulldozed track runs down the northern shore of Loch Ericht, an estate road servicing Ben Alder Lodge, six miles down the lochside. Fading yellow broom fringes the side of the track, and on the shore the white-bleached stumps of ancient pines stand as ancient monuments of long ago, mere ghosts of their former glory. This was a familiar track.

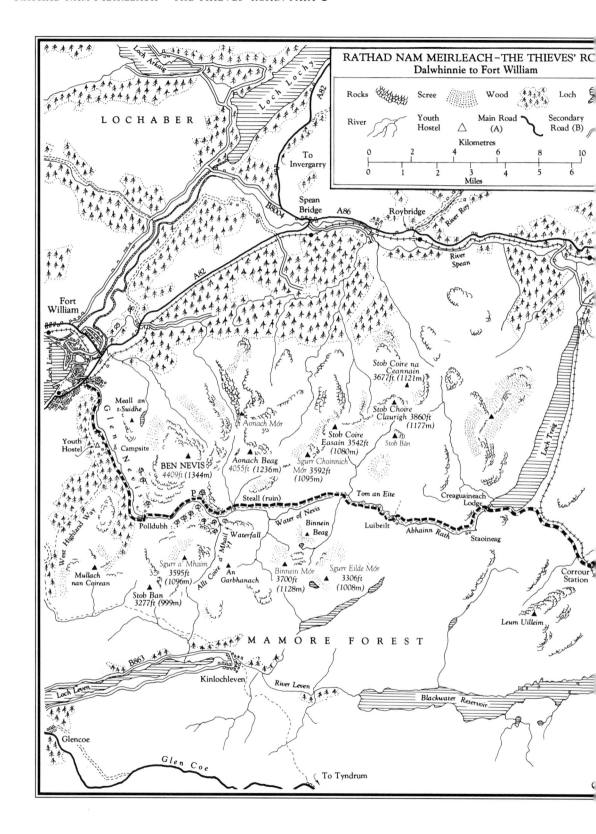

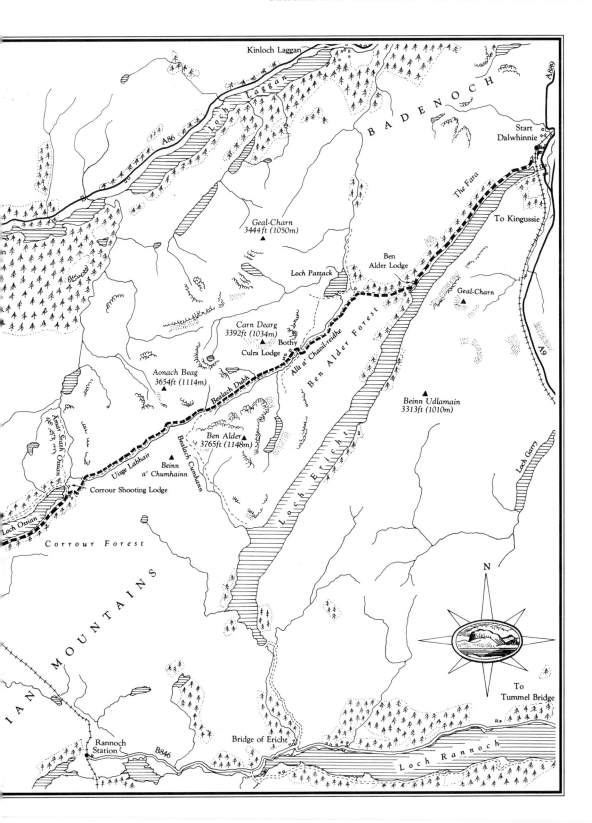

Kinloch Laggan

B A D E N O C H

Loch Laggan

A86

A889

Start
Dalwhinnie

Geal-Charn
3444ft (1050m)
▲

The Fara

To Kingussie

Ben
Alder Lodge

Loch Pattack

Geal-Charn
▲

Carn Dearg
3392ft (1034m)
▲   Bothy
Culra Lodge

Allt a' Chaoil-reidhe

Ben Alder Forest

A9

Aonach Beag
3654ft (1114m)
▲

Bealach Dubh

Beinn Udlamain
3313ft (1010m)
▲

Ben Alder ▲
3765ft (1148m)

Bealach Cumhann

Loch Ericht

Amar Srath Ossian

Beinn
a' Chumhainn
▲

Uisge Labhair

Loch Garry

Corrour Shooting Lodge

Loch Ossian

C o r r o u r   F o r e s t

N

To
Tummel Bridge

I A N   M O U N T A I N S

Rannoch
Station

B846

Bridge of Ericht

Loch Rannoch

Many is the time I have walked briskly down here in anticipation of a couple of days on Ben Alder or on the great Aonach Beag ridge, and many a time I have crawled back along it, cursing its long empty miles, footsore and weary. How great is the motivation of anticipation. A growing number of hill-goers now advocate the principle of 'the long walk in'. On hills that are easy of access, the problems of over-use and the resulting erosion are now very evident – you need only look at the problems of Ben Lawers in Perthshire, which has a National Trust for Scotland visitor centre and car-park at a height of 2000 feet at the very base of the hill. The erosion is appalling. Likewise, the chairlift which carries thousands of people up Cairngorm every summer has led to massive erosion on the Cairngorm plateau. Would the number of tramping boots be the same if all those people had to walk up the hill? I suspect not. The barrier of distance and effort acts as an effective 'granny stopper' and usually discourages all but the most enthusiastic.

This is an élitist attitude, no doubt about that, but I'm unashamedly élitist when it comes to preserving the precious qualities of the hills. By their very nature, the mountains of Scotland demand a certain level of physical ability and skill, and it's no coincidence that the remotest of these mountains tend to be the most respected and appreciated.

Nothing had changed on this 'long walk in' down Loch Ericht. There's the great sweep of far-flung mountain and moor as the track curves due west on to the vast flats of Pattack, and, frowning down on the entire scene, the black cliffs of Ben Alder and the Lancet Edge of Geal-Charn, their steep slopes forming the prominent notch of the Bealach Dubh ('the black pass'), the road to the west.

I had continued the walk straight on from Dalwhinnie, so had started this stretch in the late afternoon. I was ready for a campsite and, between the alluvial flats of Loch Pattack and the peat hag-ridden moor, I managed to find a dry sheltered spot for the tent. Several white horses, garrons, grazed contentedly a few yards away from the tent, adding to the dream-like quality of the place. The old head stalker of this estate, Geordie Oswald, was always quite happy for walkers to drive their cars right up here from Dalwhinnie, but warned that the garrons had an appetite for wing mirrors!

Geordie was one of the great characters of the area and retired only recently to move back to his native Aberdeenshire. He was a great friend to hill-walkers and frequently gave slide shows to walking and climbing clubs.

Charles Edward Stuart passed through here on his post-Culloden flight. Hard walking brought him from the Great Glen over the Laggan Hills and through by Loch Pattack to Ben Alder, where he was hospitably received by Cluny MacPherson, himself a Jacobite in hiding. A cave high above Loch Ericht offered shelter from his continuous struggle against the elements before word came that a French frigate awaited him off the coast of Moidart to ferry him back to France.

Pattack to Loch Treig

•

Morning brought the familiar patter of rain on the flysheet. The white garrons had deserted me with my dreams, no doubt preferring a dry stable somewhere to my diminishing stock of sugar cubes. The Bealach Dubh had vanished in a turmoil of cloud, and what had been a vibrant prospect of greens, browns and blacks the evening before had, this morning, become a solemn fusion of different shades of grey. The perfect opportunity for a lie-in.

It was after ten o'clock when I shifted myself, and my procrastinations paid off for once: the rain had stopped, and the clouds looked as though they were beginning to break up. A wet path ran alongside the slow-flowing Allt a' Chaoil-reidhe, past the bothy and empty lodge at Culra, and over the bumps and dips of the moraines that herald the beginnings of the Bealach Dubh. Through the great black jaws I climbed, to see a view of superb splendour unfolding. Far down the long glen in front of me lay the waters of Loch Ossian, named after the bardic son of the great Fionn MacCumhail, better known in Scotland as Fingal. Beyond the loch towered the mighty guardians of the west, the great peaks of the Mamore Forest, the Grey Corries and the Aonachs, and Ben Nevis itself. This must have been a welcome sight for the Lochaber raiders as they hurried home from their reiving, back into their own familiar lands.

At the foot of this long glen, just east of Loch Ossian, a clan skirmish took place in the seventeenth century. Some MacDonnells of Keppoch had set out on the caterans' road towards Speyside, intent on a raid into Moray. They had not gone far when word was brought to them that Grants from Speyside were in fact behind them in Keppoch, 'lifting' MacDonnell cattle. Infuriated, they returned without delay, caught the Grants red-handed and killed them almost to a man. The surviving Grants, a small band of three or four, escaped and made their way by Loch Treig to Loch Ossian, where they met some strangers to whom they confided that they were being pursued by 'cursed MacDonnell heathens'. Unknown to them the strangers were also MacDonnells, who saved their fellow-clansmen a long chase by dispatching the Grants to a quick and bloody grave.

Loch Ossian is remote, with no easy way to reach it, but it is not bleak. High mountains surround it, and the edges of the loch are softened by woods. A youth hostel sits on a tiny peninsula at the western end of the loch, a wooden shack of a building, with an atmosphere which is peculiar to this type of accommodation: the reek of the red-hot kitchen stove, the steamed-up windows, the boiling pots and pans, and the conversation in a dozen languages as young people of different backgrounds and creeds mix together in the relaxing beauty of a magnificent setting. The warden, Tom Rigg, was out feeding deer; we chatted for a while, me about my ten years as a youth hostel

ABOVE: The wild and relatively remote mountains of the Central Highlands,
Beinn Bheoil, Ben Alder and the Lancet Edge. The Thieves' Road runs between the latter two,
through the pass known as Bealach Dubh.

Far Right: Loch Ericht, like a long wind tunnel between the village of Dalwhinnie
and the wastes of Rannoch Moor.

Right: The white garrons of Ben Alder Lodge – they apparently enjoy eating car wing mirrors!

•

warden in Aviemore, and he about the changing face of hostels and hostellers. He remarked that he had booked in over a thousand bednights during the winter months, most of the hostellers arriving by train. He didn't know how the proposed cuts to the Glasgow–Fort William sleeper service would affect him, but feared the worst. Corrour Station is only a half-mile or so along the track and forms the portals to a weekend of freedom for many who arrive by train.

A keen hill man who comes north as often as he possibly can is Chris Smith MP. Chris is the only Member of Parliament to have climbed all the Munros and was instrumental in encouraging his pal, the late John Smith, to take up the hill game.

Unlike some climbers, Chris doesn't drive north for his hill sorties but prefers to leave Westminster at a reasonable time, take a taxi to Euston Station, and the Fort William sleeper to Tyndrum, Bridge of Orchy, Rannoch, Corrour or Tulloch, where he enjoys a couple of days in the hills before the Sunday-night sleeper deposits him back in London.

Over the years, that Friday-night sleeper has become something of a club, with London escapees making full use of the service comfortably to reach the Scottish hills, some of the finest in the country. On a number of occasions I've met the sleeper as it arrived from London. As it pulls into Corrour Station the faces peer eagerly from the doors, anticipating the weekend ahead. Some stay at Morgan's Den, the bunkhouse at Corrour; others stay at Tom's youth hostel. Some make their way over to the old bothy at Ben Alder cottage, while others simply camp out. All of them appreciate the sleeper service from London and are dumbstruck by the fact that British Rail is planning to chop it from the timetables.

Faceless accountants say it doesn't pay, but neither does the glorious West Highland Line, so does that mean one of the most wonderful rail journeys in the world will be next to go?

From Corrour a path follows the line north-westwards to the southern shores of Loch Treig, a long six-mile trough hemmed in on both sides by 3000-foot (914-m) mountains. The waters of Treig help power the aluminium factory at Fort William, which seems rather strange since Fort William is over fifteen miles away, but a long tunnel was burrowed in 1929 from here, through part of Ben Nevis, and down to the aluminium works. When it was finished it was the first tunnel of its type in the world.

I passed another empty house, Creaguaineach Lodge, crossed a bridge over the rushing waters of the Abhainn Rath, which has its source high in the bowels of the Grey Corries, just east of Ben Nevis. A small ledge high above the track, surrounded by bright patches of chickweed wintergreen, yellow primroses and butterwort, the insectivorous plants of moist ground, looked like an ideal spot for the night, and a bubbling of pure stream water nearby convinced me. Up went the tent, on went the stove, and I settled in for a good meal, a couple of drams and an early night.

Loch Treig to Fort William

•

The final seventeen or so miles to Fort William are delightful, with a heady contrast between the rich pastoral scenery of the meadows and woods below Staoineag and the bare wetlands of Tom an Eite, the watershed between Loch Treig and Glen Nevis.

I moved off early to a rousing chorus of stonechats, pipits, lapwings and tits, with a family of dippers joining me in the gentle stravaig (wander) alongside the Abhainn Rath, through glorious green meadows alive with primroses and harebells, the Scottish bluebell. Above, the river takes on its Highland aspect again, and comes crashing through the narrow gorge with desperation and rush. Sandpipers called as I passed the bothy at Staoineag on the opposite side of the river, with the outline of the Mamores and the Ben framed between the trees.

The old house at Luibeilt lay silent and desolate, even the protecting clutch of pines beside it failing to save it from the decaying ferocity of the winter winds. This is an open landscape, and the pull of the mountains is all around; on the left the great ridges of the Mamores, and on the right the Grey Corries, the bulk of the Aonachs, and the bald smooth pate of Ben Nevis dominating all.

The rough path on the northern bank of the Abhainn Rath at Luibeilt has to be swapped for the one on the southern bank, and there is no bridge; this means a ford and probably wet feet. It doesn't really matter all that much, though, because a couple of miles further on lies Tom an Eite, one of the boggiest and wettest places I know. From here down to Steall, the Water of Nevis kept me company, growing very quickly from a mere boggy puddle at Tom an Eite to a raging torrent of gargantuan proportions and power as it roars its way through the gorge from Steall to upper Polldubh. Steall itself is a fine spot, and a constant source of surprise to those who follow the path above the wooded ravine from the car-park at Polldubh. From a jumble of fallen rocks and boulders one comes across a scene of utter tranquillity, despite the crashing and thundering of the huge waterfall that drops down sheer from Allt Coire a' Mhail.

This shady and peaceful place is not without sadness, though, for a few years ago, when the cottage at Lower Steall (nowadays a climbers' hut) was a croft, the crofter was cutting hay on the meadow opposite the house when his wife sent their young daughter down to summon her father for a meal. She slipped while attempting to cross the fast-flowing river and was carried away by the current. Her body was found five miles downstream.

Below Steall, the Water of Nevis becomes a thundering cataract as it flows from the flats and gouges its way through and down a tight narrow gorge. Huge smoothed boulders fill the deep river-bed, and the waters take absolutely no notice of them, crashing,

ABOVE: END OF THE TRAIL IN GLEN NEVIS. THIS IS A FAMILIAR PLACE TO THOUSANDS OF TOURISTS WHO FLOCK TO THE WESTERN HIGHLANDS EVERY YEAR, EAGER TO SEE BEN NEVIS, THE HIGHEST HILL IN THE COUNTRY. WHILE MANY ARE HAPPY JUST TO LOOK, THOUSANDS TAKE TO THE ROCKY TRACK THAT LEADS TO THE SUMMIT.

RIGHT: THE WESTERN END OF LOCH OSSIAN, NAMED AFTER THE BARDIC WARRIOR SON OF THE LEGENDARY FIONN MACCUMHAIL.

•

surging, rumbling and roaring over, below and past them, in a mad race to reach the bottom of the glen and the open obscurity of Loch Linnhe.

A footpath eases its way down beside the gorge, hugging the wet rocky walls, a shady Himalayan look-alike which leads to the car-park at Polldubh, and the start of a five-mile stretch of tarmac road to Fort William. There is no anticlimax, though, tarmac road or not. The thundering river makes a good companion, and the gnarled pines that fringe the road are old and proud and full of character. The glen floor is well covered in birch and pine, and the road twists and undulates its way to the town, past the youth hostel, the campsite, the end of the West Highland Way, and the end of this walk. No doubt the fat Moray cattle were a few pounds slimmer by the time they were allowed to graze freely on the meadows of Glen Nevis. I think I was too.

And so too are thousands of tourists who come to Fort William and Glen Nevis every year, primarily to gaze at the lofty slopes of Ben Nevis, at 4409 feet (1344 m) the highest mountain in the UK.

Many of them take to the rocky slopes of the tourist track which runs from Achintee at the foot of Glen Nevis. This route is probably the easiest one to the summit, but it's also the least attractive. Unfortunately all the other routes call for some hill-walking expertise, and in many ways I suppose there is safety in numbers – something you won't find on the Thieves' Road.

CHAPTER ELEVEN

THE ISLE OF SKYE

THE FINEST LANDSCAPE ANYWHERE?

•

Richard Else

MAP: *OS 1:50 000 Sheet 32, but this is one area where a larger-scale map is essential: 1: 25 000*
Outdoor Leisure Sheet 8
START AND FINISH: *The northern end of Loch Slapin. Grid Ref: 561222*
LENGTH: *19 miles (30 km)*
APPROXIMATE TIME: *2–3 days*
TERRAIN: *A variety of mountain scenery with no real difficulties for experienced walkers*
ACCOMMODATION: *At Elgol, Broadford and Sligachan. Camping at Sligachan and Broadford*
TRANSPORT: *A post bus departs from Broadford for Elgol in the morning, returning early afternoon. A regular bus*
service links Kyle of Lochalsh and Broadford, while a more infrequent service runs between Armadale and
Broadford. Timetables vary according to the season

I once read that Scotland has no fewer than 787 islands, and that's if you restrict the count to those that can be inhabited by people or, more realistically, can afford sufficient vegetation for one or more sheep. In other words, sea-washed skerries and sheer rock formations don't count! But out of that surprisingly large total, Skye is the one island that everyone has heard of. It is the place about which writers dig deep to come up with a whole array of superlatives in an attempt to describe the magic of the island. For there is no doubt that this particular island exerts a powerful hold over many people who come under its spell. I am pleased to count myself among those who have the incurable 'Skye disease', yet I have often felt that tourists who visit only in their coaches or cars must leave Skye feeling somewhat bewildered by their visit. For the Isle of Skye, the largest of Scotland's islands, offers some of the most awe-inspiring landscapes anywhere. Some writers have added anywhere 'in Scotland', others anywhere 'in Britain' and at least one, the legendary Ben Humble, declared that the Cuillin Hills, 'have no equal in all the world'. Yet this is a landscape that needs exploring at close quarters and not viewed simply from a car or bus window. Beneath the tourist

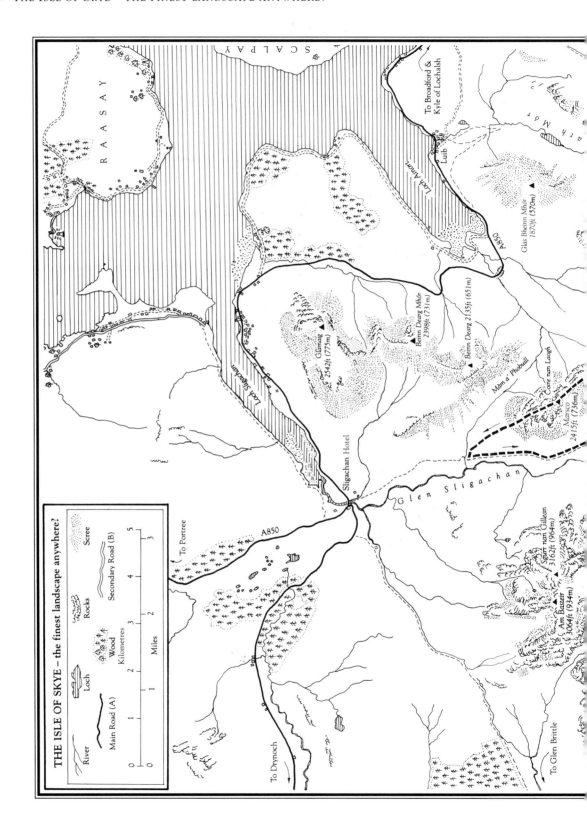

THE ISLE OF SKYE – the finest landscape anywhere?

River

Loch

Main Road (A)

Rocks

Wood

Scree

Secondary Road (B)

Kilometres

Miles

RAASAY

SCALPAY

To Broadford &
Kyle of Lochalsh

Loch Ainort

Luib

A850

Glas Bheinn Mhór
1870ft (570m)

Loch Ma...

Beinn Dearg Mhór
2398ft (731m)

Beinn Dearg 2135ft (651m)

Glamaig
2542ft (775m)

Màm a' Phobuill

Coire nam Loagh

Marsco
2415ft (736m)

Loch Sligachan

Sligachan Hotel

Glen Sligachan

A850

To Portree

Sgurr nan Gillean
3162ft (964m)

Am Basteir
3064ft (934m)

To Drynoch

To Glen Brittle

Torrin

LOCH SLAPIN

STRATH HAIRD

B8083

Elgol

N

Sgurr nan
Eag 2644ft
(806m)

Start

Bla Bheinn
3045ft (928m)

Creitheach

Loch na
Creitheach

Camasunary

Loch
nan Leachd

Camus
Fhionnairigh

Sgurr Hain

Stepping Stones

Sgurr na Stri
1630ft (497m)

The
Bad Step

Rubha Bàn

LOCH SCAVAIG

Drum Hain

Loch Coruisk

C U I L L I N   H I L L S

3192ft (973m)
Sgurr na Banachdich
3166ft (965m)

Sgurr Dearg 3234ft (986m)
Sgurr Mhic Choinnich
3110ft (948m)
Sgurr Dubh Mòr
3097ft (944m)
Sgurr Alasdair
3254ft
(992m)

Sgurr nan Eag
3031ft (924m)

Gars-bheinn
2936ft (895m)

S O A Y

myth and legend, this is a land of rugged beauty, with a climate that can be harsh and gentle within the span of a single day, and a history of mountain exploration as exciting as any in Scotland.

I first visited Skye on a cycle tour of western Scotland many years ago and suffered a fate similar to one that awaits many casual visitors. I travelled the road between Armadale and Kyleakin in thick mist, and my horizons were focused continually a few yards on the road in front. Returning three weeks later from the Outer Isles and travelling south from Uig, there were two days of driving rain. It was only afterwards that I heard the simple maxim that you stand the best chance of good weather the longer you stay on the island.

On that first visit I came with my partner Meg, and she was with me again when we came in the shorter days of the year's end to explore the outlying hills to the east of the main Cuillin Ridge. When I first met Meg she had just returned from Norway, where she had travelled through the Hardanger mountains with just a sleeping-bag and a couple of bars of chocolate. She had no map, tent, stove or many of the things that most of us think are essential. Instead, she just took her bearings from the landscape and found shelter where she could. This willingness to explore wilderness environments with the minimum of gear and equipment has always impressed me, and I have often thought that much of what we think of as essential is, in fact, merely a desirable accessory. Nowadays Meg is as happy as I am to take the new, lightweight equipment that has been developed since the early 1980s, but she still has that same smile (it spreads from virtually ear to ear) as you leave civilization behind and set out into the wilderness. In a word, it says 'freedom'.

The hills to the east of the main Cuillin Ridge are relatively neglected, and that is not surprising given that their near neighbours have attracted such attention. Today, especially at weekends, you will find a steady succession of walkers ascending Blà Bheinn in order to tick off the only Munro outside the principal group, but the other tops are comparatively quiet. Even in summer, when the tourist coaches and cars make an endless procession on the road north from Broadford, and main Cuillin is busy with walkers and climbers, I have found these eastern hills to be unfrequented in comparison.

The three-day walk we had planned covers nineteen miles, takes in three fine mountains and reveals some of the best views of the Cuillins. While we had to contend with days that were amongst the shortest of the year, we expected to meet few, if any, other walkers and knew we would be experiencing these hills in their natural state.

Getting to Skye has become a prosaic affair since the opening of the new bridge with its expensive tolls. Whether the concrete will ever blend into the landscape is a matter of some debate, but it certainly does not enhance the view seawards from the Kyle of Lochalsh. Taking the ferry across at sunset on a fine day gave a fantastic start to any visit. Now we are left with a line of tarmac and a crash barrier.

Loch Slapin to Glen Sligachan

•

Leaving the vehicle at the northern end of Loch Slapin, we made our way west by the Allt Aigeinn with a view to ascending Garbh-bheinn, which means, appropriately, 'rough mountain'. Northwards is a view up the wide U-shaped expanse of Srath Mór with Glas Bheinn Mhór seen in the far distance, while away eastwards is the small community of Torrin and the low-lying hills of the eastern part of the island. Ascending from sea-level, you have to walk every foot of the mountain's 2644 feet (806 m). Yet this is not the boring trudge it might first appear. Walking by the stream, we soon came to a small water-shoot followed by more spectacular cascades. Once the craggy wall of Sgurr nan Each on the opposite side of the glen was reached, we began the steady pull up towards the Bealach na Beiste. Initially, the impression is that this is a steep haul, but in fact the ascent is quite easy. There are also enticing views back when you pause for breath, and the higher you get the more of the mainland is revealed. From the bealach we made steady progress up a boulder and scree slope until we gained the ridge proper and followed it unerringly to the modest summit cairn. I had been here some months earlier, in the middle of summer, and then a fierce, driving wind bringing in continuous banks of mist had robbed me of any views and had made standing on the summit a precarious business. On that occasion I had started with just a thin shirt and lightweight trousers, but ended up putting on every scrap of clothing that could be found in my rucksack. Today, though, we had time to find a seat and look around this magnificent landscape. The views to Blà Bheinn and down into the Srath na Crèitheach were especially fine, but although we took immense pleasure in looking in every direction and trying to recall the names of everything we saw, the landscape served to fuel another debate.

As we unwrapped chocolate bars, cheese and oatcakes, Meg began to analyse the wilderness quality that is found in this part of Skye. The Cuillins are an intricate set of mountains, and you could spend many, many years exploring them fully, but they are also a crowded range of hills. It is only six miles from the summit of Sgurr nan Gillean along the ridge to that of Gars-bheinn, and even including the most northerly mountain in the Red Cuillins, Glamaig, adds just four miles more. Measuring west to east, say from Glen Brittle to Torrin, is just ten and a half miles. The Black Cuillins themselves occupy only about thirty square miles. Therefore, within a very small area lies an outstanding variety of mountain scenery, including remote lochs, high corries, sharp ridges and challenging summits. Meg observed that often the real wilderness in Skye exists in the glens and remote corries rather than on many of the peaks. Lower down is an inaccessible, challenging wilderness, but on a top like Garbh-bheinn the effect is different: while the panoramic view north to Scalpay and Raasay gives a sense of scale

and majesty, you can never quite forget that civilization is just around the corner with the ribbon of the A850 snaking its way from Broadford to Sligachan.

Descending from Garbh-bheinn by its northern ridge, we met the only other walker of the day. The three of us felt that despite the shorter days this was an excellent time to explore these hills, with the absence of all people adding to their mystery and grandeur. After a few additional pleasantries we went our separate ways, each of us no doubt thinking how lucky we had been to have such good weather and the hills so empty.

Our next summit was Marsco, and although it was barely mid-afternoon when we began our ascent the light was already beginning to drop. We contoured around the small hill at the bottom of the ridge (shown simply as point 489 on OS maps) and across to the bealach that led to the ascent proper.

ALTHOUGH OUR ROUTE DOESN'T ACTUALLY CLIMB ANY OF THE BLACK CUILLIN, THE PRESENCE OF THESE
WONDERFUL HILLS IS WITH YOU FOR VIRTUALLY THE ENTIRE WALK. THIS IS SGURR NAN GILLEAN, WITH THE
MORE ROUNDED TOPS OF THE RED CUILLIN TO THE LEFT.

•

The smoothness of Marsco is in stark contrast to Garbh-bheinn and clearly shows the diversion between the Black and the Red Cuillins. There is a sense, I think, in which you climb the hills in the Black Cuillins but walk those of the Red. This is not, of course, strictly accurate in the literal sense but it does give some indication of the difference between them. The Red Cuillins are composed predominantly of granite, while the Black Cuillins are made up of gabbro, a rock found nowhere else in Britain (apart from neighbouring Rhum), and its hard surface gives superb climbing, although it can easily tear your hands to shreds. As well as gabbro, the Black Cuillins consist of basalt and dolerite, and it's the erosion of these latter rocks that forms the vertical dykes and chimneys as well as the sills which are so characteristic of these mountains. Hills like Marsco, on the other hand, have a distinctly smooth profile that reflects their predominantly granite composition.

The 1312-feet (400-m) ascent to the summit of Marsco is accomplished without difficulty, and the fine views on the way up reveal many aspects of this landscape simultaneously. Away to the east the outlook to Loch Ainort and beyond contrasts with the jagged peaks of the Black Cuillins to the west. From the southern summit at 2110 feet (643 m) it is a steady climb to the true summit right in the centre of the mountain at 2415 feet (736 m). By now we were almost opposite Sgurr nan Gillean and looked across to its craggy top. It's impossible to look into the Black Cuillins without recalling the history of their exploration and the early climbers whose names will always be associated with them. I thought especially of Norman Collie, the first Professor of Chemistry at the University of London and someone who had mapped and explored these mountains in the company of a local man, John Mackenzie from Sconser. Collie made a number of visits to Skye as a young man. In later life he rented a house in Glen Brittle almost every summer, and he eventually settled on the island during the Second World War. In the twenty years from 1888 he put up a number of new routes on mountains as diverse as Sgurr nan Gillean, Sgurr Mhic Choinnich, Am Basteir, Sgurr Coir an Lochain and Sron na Ciche. Like many climbers since, he was captivated by the challenges posed by these peaks, but in his case there were no guidebooks. Often he and Mackenzie simply did not know what lay around the next corner.

Meg and I were chatting about this thrill of genuine exploration as we walked on Marsco's summit ridge. The light had by now faded even more, and the first car headlights could be seen weaving along on the road to the north. The most usual route of descent from the summit is to head just north of east and down into Coire nan Laogh and onwards to Màm a' Phobuill before turning north-west to the top of Glen Sligachan, and, other than retracing your steps, this is certainly the best way to descend from the hill. However, we decided to continue our walk north along the summit crest. I often find it hard to leave the top of a mountain and now, with the light rapidly fading, I knew we should descend without further delay. But in such good weather it was tempting to see the last glimmer of daylight from this height. We walked to the north of the ridge and then scrambled down its north-western face. Initially, the descent is pretty steep and, as so often on Skye, there is enough loose rock to make sure you take care and stay alert. In fact, I always think that one of the characteristics of walking in the Cuillins is the instability of even very large boulders. We picked our way carefully down this side of the mountain, moving from little gullies to ridges as appropriate, savouring the adventure. We seemed to be losing the light with almost every step, but not until I had put my foot on what I thought was a rock slab only to discover that its surface was a lethal combination of water and slime did we get the headtorches out of the rucksack. With the two beams making pools of light on the grass, rock and scree, we descended the last 300 or 400 feet into Glen Sligachan. No longer able to see any car headlights, we now felt part of this wilderness.

Finding a camping spot away from the worst of the boggy ground, we quickly put up the tent in darkness, aware that the wind was rising and that rain had suddenly begun to fall. Thankful for the superb design of modern tents, which were in complete contrast to those we first used many years ago, in a few minutes we had the stove roaring and made the first brew of the evening. Looking at my watch, I noticed that it was not yet half-past six, although the darkness and sense of isolation made it feel much later. As we cooked our meal (if that is the proper term for adding water to a foil pouch!) the wind picked up even more, and a fierce storm meant that we did not hear the stillness of the glen on that particular evening.

Glen Sligachan to Camasunary

•

The compensation for a noisy night was perfect settled weather the following morning when we looked up to Marsco and saw the exact line we had followed down the mountain. The route was less than perfect, however, but exciting! As we packed away the tent, we paused to look at the imposing scenery surrounding us on all sides. We were now underneath the towering mass of Sgurr nan Gillean; we could see the imposing entrance to Harta Corrie, and even small hills, like Ruadh Stac, had a presence that is more impressive when seen from below.

Our plans were to walk down Glen Sligachan but to take the path that led to one of my favourite spots in the whole of the Cuillins – Loch Coruisk. As we walked down the glen and saw successive mountains, corries and glens reveal themselves, Meg

OVERLEAF: MARSCO IN GLEN SLIGACHAN WITH SGURR NA STRI JUST POPPING ITS HEAD UP ABOVE

THE LOWER HILLS ON THE RIGHT.

•

began our second discussion on this landscape by trying to define what makes it so distinctive. Successive generations of writers have praised the Black Cuillins and spoken of their special qualities. Ben Humble, to take one obvious example, described being on the Cuillin Ridge as being 'on the very top of the world, with wondrous Hebrid panoramas all round. I cannot think of the Cuillin as black. Light grey, steel blue, rose-flushed in dawn, tipped blood-red in the evening sun – all these I have seen and many others.' Sir Walter Scott found the Cuillins more ominous; they 'appeared to consist of precipitous sheets of naked rock, down which the torrents were leaping in a hundred lines of foam. The tops of the ridge, apparently inaccessible to human foot, were rent and split into the most tremendous pinnacles.' But for Seaton Gordon 'they are inspiring on a day of storm when the grey wrack streams through their corries where the eagle soars and the raven drifts like a miniature eagle above the highest summit'. Like many walkers and climbers in the last hundred years and more, I have always been pulled to this landscape – and I am thinking here of all of the Cuillins – but have never been quite sure how to define that attraction. Meg had been reading Alexander Smith's *A Summer in Skye* which was first published in 1865 and did much to enhance the popularity of the island. Today it is still worth reading his book, not as an accurate historical account of nineteenth-century life on Skye, but as a work that is outstanding in capturing the spirit of the place. Smith perhaps does that best of all in describing Glen Sligachan. It is, he says, a place where 'the scenery drives you in on yourself. The enormous bulks of the mountains, their austere silence, daunt you, and you hardly care to speak lest you be overheard. You cannot laugh; you would not crack a joke for the world. Glen Sligachan would be a place to do a little self-examination in.' Today we might not share his sense of melodrama, but there is no denying that Glen Sligachan is the most imposing of glens and the walk to Loch Coruisk probably without equal.

Taking the right-hand fork where Glen Sligachan meets Srath na Crèitheach, we wound our way upwards to the bealach between Druim Hain and Sgurr Hain. In the three and a half miles it had taken us to reach here, we had been impressed constantly by all aspects of this wilderness. On the one hand we found our eyes drawn consistently to the jagged shape of the Cuillin Ridge which was always evolving as we made our way southwards. On the other hand there was just as much pleasure in the colours of ferns by the side of a stream or in the light reflected in the lochans. Once at the bealach there is a desire to keep moving and walk down towards Loch Coruisk. On the Sunday morning of our walk, the whole Cuillin Ridge was incredibly peaceful, with hardly a breath of wind remaining from the previous evening's storm. This route is one of the oldest in the area and is marked on Bartholomew's map from the early part of the century, but that morning we saw no one as we picked our way down to the loch. I often think of Loch Coruisk as the inner sanctuary of the Black Cuillins, a feeling that comes, I think, from its remote location. The easiest route, if the longest, is to walk in from the north; otherwise there is the path from Camasunary in the east or the hiring of a boat from Elgol to arrive across Loch Scavaig.

Standing at the eastern end of the loch is a magical experience which, of course, is partly due to the superb views of Sgurr Alasdair and its neighbouring peaks. Sgurr Alasdair was named after the Skyeman, Sheriff Alexander Nicolson, who made the first ascent in 1873. In fact, Skye is one of the few places in Britain where you can find peaks named after climbers, although the larger peaks were named long before by the local people. But it's not just the mountains, magnificent as they are, that give Loch Coruisk its distinctive identity. Two recent large rockfalls, one on either side of the water, confirm that even the most rugged landscape is always undergoing changes, but, nevertheless, this place has a sense of primeval splendour. To my mind the dramatic effect of the ice in scooping out the rock to make this corrie of water gives it such a haunting setting and perhaps now, at the beginning of winter, with no other walkers about and the light a steely grey, this is the best time at which to see the loch.

We could have lingered here for many hours exploring the lochside and the River Scavaig that runs just a few hundred yards from the loch to the sea, but after an impromptu lunch of the remaining cheese and oatcakes it was time to move onwards. Walking east along the coast path, I looked at Loch nan Leachd and remembered coming here nearly ten years earlier and seeing dozens of seals bathing on the rocks that lie just off the coast. Then I was in a small boat, and we were able to get very close before the seals finally found our presence intrusive and slipped into the water. Today, though, these rocks were deserted as we began to make our way along the path and towards 'the Bad Step', an awkward bit of rock that has achieved a status of its own over the years, and is unusual in being named as such on OS maps. In the late 1960s it was the subject of controversy when plans were unveiled to make access easier to this remote area. Part of the project involved the dynamiting of the Bad Step, and the plans were halted only after a public outcry. Today the Bad Step is there in all its glory, although the difficulty of crossing it is mainly a mental one: it poses no real problems, as the rock is sound, but you do have to commit yourself to launching out on what, from this direction at least, is a convex curve with the sea plunging away some twenty or so feet below. On a wet day and with a full pack, crossing the rock is not for the timid, but our crossing was uneventful. The rewards for circumnavigating the Bad Step outweigh all the difficulties for, as you continue along the path, splendid views to the south are revealed.

We were blessed with especially good light in which to see the nearby island of Soay (where Gavin Maxwell tried to establish a shark fishery after the last war) and the magnificent outline of Rhum. Further to the east is Eigg, and in the gap between that island and Rhum I think we also caught sight of Muck in the distance. We kept being enticed back to this view as we made our way around the headland and to the bay of Camasunary. This is one of my favourite coastal spots in the whole of Scotland,

Blà Bheinn from the north. The route described up this mountain is
from the easier south side. The mountain is owned by the John Muir Trust and so
safeguards its future in perpetuity.

•

and a good place at any time of year, but especially in the shorter days of winter, in which to put up a tent. You can spend many happy hours exploring inland to Loch na Crèitheach or along the coastline itself, with its vast array of flotsam and jetsam from places near and far, or you can simply sit with a brew looking out on a scene of timeless beauty. Talking to Meg, we both felt that between Loch Coruisk and here you have eased yourself totally into a wilderness of sea and rock. I think that this is one of the hardest places in Scotland to leave. It is a place of seclusion, a haven far removed from the modern world. Whereas Loch Coruisk has a setting that is awe-inspiring, Camasunary has a fertile, gentle beauty that gives it a peacefulness that you do not find in the main Cuillins themselves. It is a place in which to linger and watch the sun go down and the moon come up.

Camasunary to Blà Bheinn
•

Next morning we embarked on the last part of our walk. Meg, who normally gets depressed at the thought of returning to the other world once more, made the point that each day of this walk is different and each has its own highlight. Today that highlight was right in front of us – Blà Bheinn, one of the finest mountains on the whole of Skye and yet one of the easiest to ascend. As we walked up its splendid ridge, scrambling here and there as the mood took us, we enjoyed the views across Strathaird, out to the islands and west to Srath na Crèitheach with its loch immediately underneath us. This was one of those perfect sharp days when you seem almost to see for ever, and although we revelled in the tremendous views we were also thinking about the land upon which we had been walking. Coincidentally, it was almost a year to the day since the John Muir Trust had, in a bold initiative, purchased the Strathaird Estate and by doing so, safeguarded its future in perpetuity. Those last two words – in perpetuity – are what really matter. While many of us may walk for scores of years, all true hill-goers have the desire for the landscape to be safeguarded long after we have ceased to take enjoyment from it. Both of us were pleased that the John Muir Trust had been successful in its latest purchase, for out of all the public conservation bodies this one seems to be taking the most level-headed approach and adopting a coherent long-term strategy. Like the Scots-born conservationist it has taken its name from, I think the trust represents a fresh, even visionary view of how wild places should be managed. In 1991 the trust had purchased the neighbouring Torrin Estate, but with Strathaird it has acquired an estate that goes right into the heart of the Cuillins and includes not just Blà Bheinn but also Marsco, the north-eastern half of Loch Coruisk and the Elgol peninsula. Keith Miller, the trust's conservation manager, has spent his first twelve months gathering information and obtaining the co-operation and involvement of tenants and non-tenants alike who live and work in the area. This human element is fundamental to the trust's philosophy and is what sets it apart from many other conservation bodies. We all owe the JMT an enormous debt of gratitude, and it deserves our whole-hearted support.

In fact, every hill-walker who enjoys this magnificent landscape should think seriously of joining the John Muir Trust and supporting its work. The trust has acted courageously in ensuring that Strathaird and precious places like it are not simply saved for ourselves and future generations, but (and this is the difficult bit) are also managed in a sensitive way to reflect the needs of both those who work and live in this magnificent landscape and those who come here to enjoy its rocks, glens, burns, corries and ridges.

As we climbed up Blà Bheinn's ridge, we recalled that we had seen only one other person since we set out and no one at all in the last forty-eight hours. On the higher part of the ridge was a smattering of fresh snow and our bootprints were the only marks in it. As we reached the southern summit in a rising wind, we experienced the superb conditions that make this one of the finest views in the Cuillins. To the west was the vast panorama of the main Cuillin Ridge; to the south Rhum and Eigg looked better than ever. Ahead was a short but exciting scramble to the main summit that is a mere six feet or so higher: the southern one tops out at 3038 feet (926 m), while the true summit is 3045 feet (928 m). The name Blà Bheinn appears to be a mixture of Norse and Gaelic and probably means 'blue mountain'. This is appropriate, given its composition of gabbro together with dolerite and basalt and today blues and grey were definitely the predominant colours. After a couple of hours' effort going steadily upwards, we nevertheless greeted this summit ridge with very mixed feelings. For us the route lay not simply downwards but also marked a return to civilization. However interesting the path through Coire Uaigneich is, there is no denying that the wilderness is almost over. Now it is a downward walk back to the road and the waiting vehicle.

Later, over a meal and coffee in café further south on the mainland, Meg summed up both our moods perfectly. 'You see,' she said, 'there'll be some people who enjoy returning to civilization.' After a pause she added wistfully: 'Myself, I just can't understand that.'

CHAPTER TWELVE

THE CAIRNGORMS

THE LIVING MOUNTAINS

•

Cameron McNeish

A three- to four-day walk around the high tops of the Cairngorms

---

MAPS: *OS 1:50 000 Sheets 36 and 43*
START: *Tomintoul, on the A939. Grid Ref: 170187*
FINISH: *Achlean, Glen Feshie. Grid Ref: 852976*
LENGTH: *45 miles (72 km)*
APPROXIMATE TIME: *3–4 days*
TERRAIN: *A long mountain walk over the highest landscape in the country*
ACCOMMODATION: *Bothies can't be relied on for accommodation – they may be busy. You are strongly advised to carry a tent and full backpacking equipment, a sleeping-bag, insulating mat, food and something to cook it on, spare food and spare clothes. Tomintoul has a good range of hotels, guest-houses and a youth hostel. Kincraig, Kingussie and Aviemore have lots of hotels, guest-houses, b&bs, and there are bunkhouses at Glen Feshie, Kingussie and Newtonmore. If you feel like luxuriating in an enormous, well-cooked meal at the end of the walk, try eating at the Ossian Hotel, Kincraig: highly recommended. There is both a Chinese and an Indian restaurant in Aviemore, but if you really want to treat yourself in relaxing surroundings try La Taverna in Aviemore. This is an Italian restaurant of the highest order, and the difference between the food served there and the freeze-dried stuff you've been living on is too enormous to contemplate*

Someone once wrote that the Promised Land always lies on the other side of a wilderness. If this is true, then I suppose it could be interpreted as meaning that most of us who walk in wild places are in search of something. Are our sorties into the hills, moors and forests an end in themselves, or are we really looking for something deeper, more meaningful, longer-lasting? The whole subject of wilderness is a fascinating one and I'm beginning to realize that everybody has his or her own definition of the word. I don't know how many times I've been told that we have no wilderness in the UK, that everywhere we look, even in the remoter parts of the Scottish Highlands, there is evidence of man. But surely that is the case

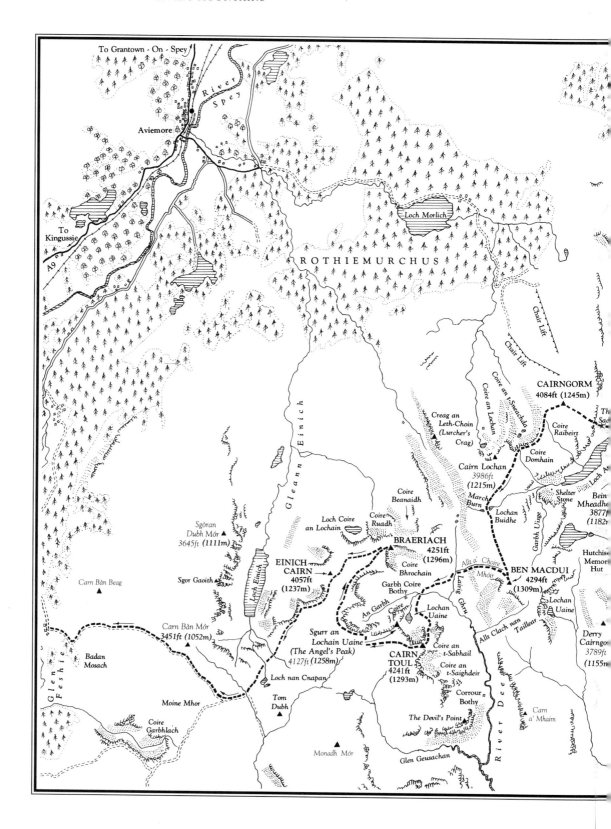

To Grantown - On - Spey

River Spey

Aviemore

To Kingussie

A9

Loch Morlich

ROTHIEMURCHUS

Chair Lift

Chair Lift

CAIRNGORM
4084ft (1245m)

Coire an t-Sneachda

Coire an Lochan

Creag an
Leth-Choin
(Lurcher's
Crag)

The
Sad

Coire
Raibeirt

Coire
Domhain

Cairn Lochan
3986ft
(1215m)

Shelter
Stone

Bein
Mheadh
3877
(1182)

Gleann Einich

Coire
Beanaidh

March
Burn

Loch A

Sgòran
Dubh Mór
3645ft (1111m)

Loch Coire
an Lochain

Coire
Ruadh

Lochan
Buidhe

Garbh Uisge

Sgor Gaoith

EINICH
CAIRN
4057ft
(1237m)

BRAERIACH
4251ft
(1296m)

Coire
Bhrochain

Allt a' Choire
Mhóir

BEN MACDUI
4294ft
(1309m)

Hutchis
Memori
Hut

Carn Bàn Beag

Garbh Coire
Bothy

An Garbh

Lairig Ghru

Lochan
Uaine

Carn Bàn Mór
3451ft (1052m)

Coire
Lochan
Uaine

Allt Clach nan
Taillear

Derry
Cairngo
3789ft
(1155m

Glen Feshie

Badan
Mosach

Sgurr an
Lochain Uaine
(The Angel's Peak)
4127ft (1258m)

CAIRN
TOUL
4241ft
(1293m)

Coire an
t-Sabhail

Coire an
t-Saighdeir

Loch nan Cnapan

Moine Mhor

Tom
Dubh

Corrour
Bothy

Carn
a' Mhaim

Coire
Garbhlach

The Devil's Point

River Dee

Monadh Mór

Glen Geusachan

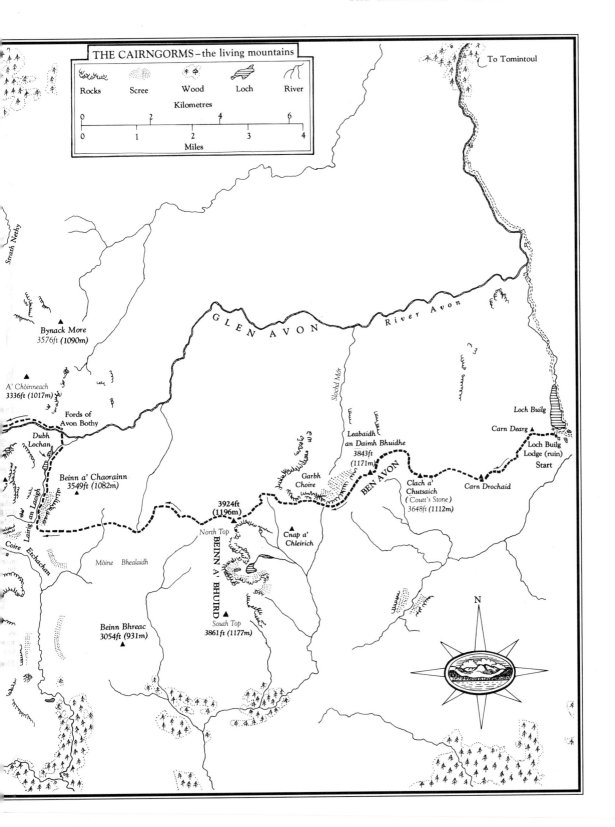

THE CAIRNGORMS – the living mountains

Rocks	Scree	Wood	Loch	River

Kilometres

0 — 2 — 4 — 6

0 — 1 — 2 — 3 — 4

Miles

To Tomintoul

G L E N   A V O N   River Avon

Strath Nethy

Bynack More
3576ft (1090m)

A' Chòinneach
3336ft (1017m)

Fords of
Avon Bothy

Dubh
Lochan

Beinn a' Chaorainn
3549ft (1082m)

Lairig an Laoigh

Coire Etchachan

Slochd Mòr

Leabaidh
an Daimh Bhuidhe
3843ft
(1171m)

Garbh
Choire

BEN AVON

Loch Builg

Carn Dearg

Loch Builg
Lodge (ruin)
Start

Clach a'
Chutsaich
(Coutt's Stone)
3648ft (1112m)

Carn Drochaid

3924ft
(1196m)

North Top

BEINN A' BHUIRD

Môine   Bhealaidh

Cnap a'
Chleirich

Beinn Bhreac
3054ft (931m)

South Top
3861ft (1177m)

N

even in many of those areas of the world that we consider to be true wilderness? You will find evidence of Indian man in many of the wilderness areas of the United States. Go to Alaska and you will find evidence of Aleut, Eskimo, Tlingit and Abathascan man. Travel in Africa and you will realize just how populated the Cradle of Humanity has been in times gone by. Even the mighty Himalaya is criss-crossed with age-old trade routes.

I had lived for a number of years in the shadow of the Cairngorms and had wandered around their delectable summits more times than I care to remember before I saw these hills as wilderness, before I even realized I was searching for something more, and I have the poetess Nan Shepherd to thank for removing the blindfold. Her writings made me realize that so much of my wandering was self-centred, I was seeking a sensuous gratification, looking for the sensations of the hills, the height, the grandeur, the feeling of physical achievement, the lust of pride. I wasn't interested in the mountain for itself, as a wilderness. I was treating the hill as a racetrack, at other times as a solace – but always I was looking to take from it.

It was Nan Shepherd who introduced me to the living mountain, to the fact that a mountain is made up of a number of component parts, each one a study in itself – its contours, its water, its rock, its flowers and birds – and that the important thing is nothing as crass as 'conquering the mountain' or 'communing with nature', but in simply being there. It's a lesson I'm learning still. She suggests that people want sensation from the mountain; they want the startling view, the horrid pinnacle – sips of beer and tea instead of milk. And while there is nothing wrong with sensation, and even less wrong with sips of beer, often the mountain gives itself most completely when you have no destination, when you reach nowhere in particular, but have gone out merely to be with the mountain as one visits a friend with no intention but to be with him or her.

Loch Builg to Cairngorm

•

After twenty-odd years of Cairngorm-wandering I have grown in familiarity with all the mountains, but sometimes there are lesser-known corners which surprise me by their character. Loch Builg has a melancholy air which is far from unattractive. The loch lies like a pool of quicksilver in a high Grampian cradle. At its far end, the outline of Loch Builg Lodge is a skeleton etched against the hillside, a sad remnant of its former glory, belonging to a past world. A lonely place now, the ruin wasn't always cloaked in quietude. These crofts and farms and shooting-lodges of the north-east Highlands bred men of character – gritty, couthy (down-to-earth), tough, thrawn (determined) – and the agricultural and sporting heritage of Aberdeenshire and Buchan and Banffshire and Moray is a craggy, granite, hard-nosed one, a heritage of savage elements, of bothans (shelters where the farm workers lived) and forty-six-verse ballads. You have to be tough in perseverance to be a north-east crofter, or a singer of north-east ballads.

I had wandered in from Tomintoul, six miles or so of easy track, easing myself into the Arctic scale of these big hills. These Grampians don't compare with anything else. No soaring pinnacles here, no serrated peaked horizons. These are rounded hills, but big hills, on a scale that takes a while to grasp.

Over supper, as the waters of the loch rippled gently under a light breath of wind, I checked my route for the next three days – and for the thousandth time in twenty-odd years gulped again at such an audacious scale of things. Three days which would take me over the six highest Cairngorm tops, over three very different high plateaux, over the largest tracts of land over 2000, 3000 and 4000 feet (610–1220 m) in the country, and three days which would undoubtedly confirm to me that these are the finest backpacking hills in Britain.

The lie of the land is kind to the expedition planner for this particular ploy. The six tops break up evenly into three days of two tops apiece: Ben Avon and Beinn a' Bhuird on the first day, the classic traverse from Cairngorm to Ben Macdui on the second, and the superb high-level route across Cairn Toul and Braeriach on the last day, before dropping down through the Rothiemurchus Forest to finish in Aviemore, or, alternatively, over the wide and empty quarter of the Moine Mhor to Glen Feshie. Some walkers take longer to walk this route, poking around and peering in corners, visiting other Cairngorm tops, while others walk it in a much shorter time, even inside twenty-four hours – the slackpackers and the power-hikers, it just depends on what game you want to play.

Loch Builg lies at the eastern extremity of Ben Avon, a hill that is almost a mountain range in itself. It's a big, complex mass of muscley shoulders that bulge out in every direction, throwing up a series of tor-studded tops. The name of the hill, Avon, is taken from the river that scours its northern flanks, and Celtic scholars believe the name to be a derivative of Ath-fhionn, 'the bright, or fair-haired one'. Local legend claims that the wife of Fionn MacCumhail, or Fingal, slipped when crossing the river and was swept to her death. The name has absolutely no connection with Shakespeare's Stratford, and it is correctly pronounced A'an.

A rough path threads an elusive route westwards from the ruin of Loch Builg Lodge and climbs the heather slopes of Carn Dearg, Ben Avon's eastern outlier. I abandoned the path and took to an area of high moorland, led on by the melancholy crooning of a golden plover, the bird of the high, lonely places. The path becomes sketchy hereabouts anyway as it climbs more steeply until the great granite wart of Clach a' Chutsaich, or Coutt's Stone, comes into view. Like most of these Cairngorm hills, Ben Avon keeps its real secrets exclusively for those who take the trouble to find them. It is

Above: Loch Avon, pronounced A'an, the jewel of the Cairngorms. In its deep-set trench between Beinn Mheadhoin and the slopes of Cairngorm, it has a real air of solitude. The route described over the high Cairngorms passes this fine viewpoint by the Féith Buidhe.

Far Left: Looking towards Cairn Toul from Braeriach. The high-level walk from Cairn Toul, over Sgurr an Lochain Uaine, to Braeriach is one of the great outings of the Cairngorms and is included in the walk described. It offers the walker a vivid impression of arctic plateau, with all the associated flora and bird life.

Left: Ptarmigan, the grouse of the high tops. This bird of the Arctic is found in abundance on the Cairngorm plateaux.

not a hill to be gazed up to, but rather a hill to gaze down from, north and west towards her Cairngorm sisters, the great rounded tops, scoured and shattered by glaciation and cleft by great ravines and corries, cliff-girt trenches and high lochans.

From Coutt's Stone an easy high-level crescent takes you around the gravelly plateau to the summit of the mountain, Leabaidh an Daimh Bhuidhe ('the couch of the yellow deer') at 3843 feet (1171 m). Immediately west of the summit, the plateau abruptly ends. Huge cornices often hang out over the edge here, with a steep drop into the great Garbh Choire ('rough corrie'). Our route to Beinn a' Bhuird lies across the top of this big corrie, and along a narrow, rocky ridge known locally as the Sneck, from the Gaelic snaig, or 'notch'. Great corries fall away on either side, and it's a superb position with rock buttresses soaring up to the green slopes of Cnap a' Chleirich to the south-west.

The summit of Beinn a' Bhuird (pronounced 'ben-a-voord') is distinctly uninteresting. It lies some 3924 feet (1196 m) above sea-level, but more often than not clouds drench these high parts and visibility is limited to a few rock-strewn feet. In conditions like these, good, sharp navigation is vital. Ask yourself a couple of elementary questions. How many paces do you take to every hundred metres, and how long does it take you to walk a kilometre? In areas like these, especially in winter and spring, pacing and timing are essential navigational tools, and if you don't know how to use these skills you could be in for a tough time.

However, when conditions are good the next stretch of the walk offers some superlative views of the rest of these Cairngorm mountains. As you descend from the summit to the broad, high level moorland below, your gaze is taken into the very bowels of Coire Etchachan, while Ben Macdui, Britain's second-highest mountain, lies dead ahead.

The deep trench of the Lairig an Laoigh separates the Avon/a' Bhuird massif from the central hills, just as the Lairig Ghru divides the next hills from the last day's walk on the western massif. These two great glens cut a swath across the granite uplands of the Cairngorms, both of them long and distinct mountain passes of essential grandeur. The story goes that cattle-drovers once took their beasts through the rough defile of the Lairig Ghru, but the younger kye were taken through the easier Lairig an Laoigh, hence its name, the 'pass of the calves, or stirks'.

Our route takes us northwards through the Lairig an Laoigh to the River Avon, to the very spot where Fingal apparently lost his wife. On the far side of the river there is a howff, a stone emergency shelter. It's generally a dirty midden of a place and is a sad testament to the walkers who pass through here and leave their rubbish behind. I'd like to see it demolished, just as Jean's Hut, the Sinclair Memorial Hut, and other Cairngorm shelters have been demolished. This place, the Fords of Avon Bothy and Corrour Bothy in the Lairig Ghru are living on borrowed time, thanks to the louts who have turned them into something ugly.

If you're going to camp, don't stop here, but follow the river to where it flows out of Loch Avon. This is one of the most precious jewels in the Cairngorm crown. I've often lain outside a tent beside this loch, where the clear waters are apparently haunted by a water horse, or kelpie. The situation is remote, with the great square-cut bulk of the Shelter Stone crag dominating the far end of the loch. Hemmed in between Beinn Mheadhoin and Cairngorm itself, Loch Avon, with the great slabs of the Garbh Uisge providing watercourses for thousands of tons of water, has the atmosphere of a great natural cathedral, with the open sky forming a painted ceiling.

An alternative start to the following day could be a walk right around the loch, but on this trip I wanted to wet my feet in the infant River Avon, and start out on a big climb towards Cairngorm, the third of the big six.

Cairngorm to Ben Macdui

•

On the north side of Loch Avon, the Saddle, a low bealach between the slopes of A' Chòinneach and Cairngorm, offers the best start to the climb. A rough path runs up the slope from the lochside to the col, which separates the Loch Avon basin from the long glen of Strath Nethy. I'm a great believer in getting the worst of the hard work finished early in the day, and that was certainly the case on that day. I arrived at the summit of Cairngorm hot and sweaty, as the mists rolled back to reveal the relative gentleness of the rest of the day's activity. I say relative, for this scenery is far from gentle, however easy the walking may be in terms of effort. This high-level walk from Cairngorm to Ben Macdui is one of the classic trade routes of the Highlands, one that rarely drops below 3000 feet (914 m). It is well marked by a worn footpath, and unnecessarily emblazoned with cairns over the rougher parts, but, if you have time, deviate from the path to enjoy the wild views down towards Loch Avon, or down into the great scalloped scoops of Coire an t-Sneachda and Coire an Lochan. A weather-station adorns the summit of Cairngorm, a squat stone building which has been buffeted and battered by some of the strongest winds to hit this country; 100-m.p.h. gales are common. It's sobering to realize that on such occasions human life is not compatible. An instructor from Glenmore Lodge told me that he had heard a wind approaching like a steam train. Reacting from impulse, he threw himself on the ground and dug his ice-axe into the snow, but when the force of the wind hit him it lifted him up and moved him several feet. That's breezy!

At 4084 feet (1245 m) Cairngorm is the fifth-highest hill in the country, and a fine viewpoint. Sadly, Macdui disappoints from this angle, appearing merely as a rise in the far terrain. But Macdui's splendours have yet to come, for it keeps its glory for those

Above: Spring snow on the high tops of the Cairngorms. From the slopes of
Cairngorm itself, looking across the deep trench that holds Loch Avon towards Loch
Etchachan. Ben Macdui appears as a rounded top with the sharper peaks of Cairn Toul and
Sgurr an Lochain Uaine to its right.

Left: Loch Einich, almost a mirror image of Loch Avon, seen from the edge of the
Moine Mhor, the Great Moss.

•

who penetrate these Cairngorm hills and not for those who take the soft option of the chairlift to the top of Cairngorm. This chairlift and the rest of the ski development on Cairngorm is cause for much debate. There is little doubt that it is ugly and environmentally displeasing, but that is the price we pay for a ski development in an area where natural regeneration is very, very slow. A much more insidious threat is the erosion caused by feet on areas like the Cairngorm/Macdui plateau and, even more recently, the Cairngorm to Loch Avon routes down to the Saddle, down Coire Raibeirt and Coire Domhain. The pressure has been brought about because of the easy access provided by a chairlift which operates all year round.

The Cairngorm plateau is a good place on which to linger. In high summer you are likely to see dotterel, that semi-tame bird of the high Arctic, snow bunting, ptarmigan, peregrine and very possibly golden eagle. The path from Cairngorm to Ben Macdui is an obvious one, but I like to wander off it, just beyond Coire Domhain, to where the slopes of Ben Macdui hurl themselves downwards to Loch Avon. This view of the loch is one of the finest in Scotland. Here the waters of the Allt Buidhe run through great cornices and snow tunnels before tumbling down red granite slabs to the loch below. Close by lie the great cliffs of Stag Rocks and the Hell's Lum crags, and to the right are the precipices of the Shelter Stone crag, looking incredibly steep and sustained from this angle.

I didn't linger too long here that morning, for there was still a fair bit of walking to be done. It is a gentle stroll along the waters of the Allt Buidhe and in the warm summer sunshine it's a beautiful walk. But the weather isn't always so benevolent. A party of schoolchildren died here in 1971 in a blinding snowstorm, a salutary reminder of how conditions up here can kill. And yet when the sun shines and the snow bunting trills out its beautiful song, it's hard to imagine the terrible times of a Cairngorm blizzard. Hard too to imagine that you're sitting at almost 4000 feet (1220 m) above sea-level.

The wander up Macdui is straightforward enough: across a boulder field, with a line of cairns marking the route like urban traffic cones. Damn the folk who build these pernicious emblems of urban man. A short gravelly climb takes you on to an upper plateau, vivid in pink screes, and on to a final rise leading to the southern summit of Macdui. At 4294 feet (1309 m), it's the second-highest mountain in the UK and the reputed lair of Ferlas Mor, the Great Grey Man. It was Professor Norman Collie, one of the leading lights of the early Alpine Club, who began the stories of the Grey Man back at the beginning of the century. This illustrious scientist, the epitome of the Victorian gentleman, told a Scottish Mountaineering Club dinner of a ten-foot-high spectral figure who takes one footstep in the crunchy snow to two of a human's, a haunting figure which follows you until fear takes a grip and you flee for fear of your life. It's all good stuff – wonderful tales for the candlelit bothy nights.

From the summit of Macdui I took stock, for the great trench of the Lairig Ghru separates the western hills of the Cairngorms, Cairn Toul and Braeriach, and, beyond, the vast Moine Mhor and the Glen Feshie hills. I wasn't too sure whether to stay the night at Corrour, deep in the bowels of the Lairig Ghru, or camp somewhere more convenient. Since Corrour is generally no better than a rural midden, I opted for a camp, making my itinerary just a bit simpler. The direct descent from Macdui into Lairig is a steep boulder slope, but, a bit south of the summit, the Allt Clach nan Taillear has formed a shallow corrie, and a very rough path leads down towards Corrour. But I wanted to take advantage of using my tent at the mouth of the An Garbh Coire, 'the big rough corrie', which is surrounded on three sides by Cairn Toul, Sgurr an Lochain Uaine and Braeriach. So I went north from Macdui and descended by the stream known as the Allt a' Choire Mhóir, which brought me out close to the infant River Dee.

Cairn Toul and Braeriach

•

Having spent the night close to the tiny rocky howff of An Garbh Coire, in which two walkers must have slept cheek by jowl, so cramped and confined is the living space in this rough shelter, I awoke to the prospect of a long, steep pull up on to Cairn Toul. It's a tough haul first thing in the morning, when the back is stiff from a hard bed, and the legs and the brain are still disconnected by the early hour. The consolation was that once I was up there I would be up for the rest of the day, and, although this ascent of Cairn Toul is steep and rocky by its north-east ridge, it offers spectacular views which improve every minute. And half-way up, the lochan (which Cairn Toul shares with Sgurr an Lochain Uaine) makes a welcome, and scenic, rest spot.

Cairn Toul, at 4241 feet (1293 m), is one of the more shapely of the Cairngorm summits, a Madonna in a land of bulging breasts. When viewed from the west it appears broad and stunted – hence 'the hill of the barn'. But from the south and east it is the most pointed of the Cairngorms, almost a Sgurr rather than a pile of stones. From the airy eyrie of its summit, a lovely high-level ridge traces its way around to form the rim of An Garbh Coire and one of the best high-level walks of Scotland.

Coming off Cairn Toul, you climb again to Sgurr an Lochain Uaine ('hill of the green lochan'), which is generally Anglicized to Angel's Peak, no doubt to compensate for Devil's Point further down the Lairig. Devil's Point is a crude but polite translation of the Gaelic: Pod nam Deathain literally means 'the penis of the devil'. The wandering mind can dwell easily on what Angel's Peak is supposed to mean.

Enjoy this high-level ramble around the red screes and you realize why these hills were once known as an Monadh Ruadh ('the red hills'). The great cliffs of Braeriach are seamed and riven by gullies and cracks, one of these containing the sprightly waters of the infant River Dee, the sparkling burn beginning a long journey which will see it become one of the major rivers of Scotland as it flows out past Balmoral and

WALKING ACROSS THE MOINE MHOR, THE GREAT MOSS, AT THE END OF THE ROUTE.
SGOR GAOITH IS IN THE DISTANCE.

•

Royal Deeside to the oil-rich fields of the North Sea at Aberdeen. Braeriach is only a short hop from here, the summit lying on the very edge of a precipice. This 'bridled upland' is 4251 feet (1296 m) in height and is the third-highest hill in the country. It's a wonderful mountain, with seven great corries gouged out of her flanks, the exploration of which, in one long scramble, makes a superb high-level expedition.

The route now leads across yet another high plateau, westwards towards the natural dereliction and peat hags of the Moine Mhor and the Glen Feshie hills. If transport can be arranged to collect you in Glen Feshie, I would urge you to experience the open spaciousness of this great moss – a land of dotterel and ptarmigan, red deer and the golden eagle. Below lies the great trench of Gleann Einich, and I've often sat on the edge of the high plateau in autumn and listened to the primeval sounds of the deer stag rut and the great roars as they challenge those who would seek to steal their harem, mixed all the while with the sweet cacophony of migrating geese as the great skeins fly in formation southwards. This is a place in which to linger, but perhaps the anticipated fleshpots of Aviemore are pulling at your heartstrings or your throats, and that first pint suddenly doesn't seem so far away.

So it's over Carn Bàn Mór, down the fox-hunters' path to Achlean, where, hopefully, a waiting car will whisk you off to the first watering-hole. Three miles down the glen a private bunkhouse offers accommodation for those without transport, from where a taxi can be telephoned, or you can gird your loins in anticipation of another few miles' walk to Kincraig.

POSTSCRIPT

OTHER JOURNEYS, OTHER TIMES

•

Richard Else

As the years go by, many of us find it harder to get away. We get tied to our routines; to jobs; to commitments; even to our phones, faxes and e-mail. Not to mention the World Wide Web... The irony in all this, of course, is that travel is now easier than ever and its cost, relatively speaking, cheaper. There is also an almost infinite number of places you can go to and experience something of the true wilderness.

Sometimes this can be a scene of breathtaking beauty which makes an immediate impact. Some years ago I remember a small group of us trekking up the Diamar valley in Pakistan's Punjab Himalaya. For four days or so we had been walking further into the mountains. Photographing and walking, we had moved steadily into a remote region of small villages that had been precariously established on little pockets of flat land that clung to the mountainside. Then, early one morning, after the routine of striking camp and easing into the usual more or less rhythmical pace, I was stopped literally in my tracks. It was before eight o'clock and I had not yet fully woken to the day, but there straight ahead, but still at a distance, was the inestimable bulk of Nanga Parbat. Looking for the first time at one of the world's great mountains rendered me speechless as I tried to grapple simultaneously with so many thoughts. There was no sense of scale, no sense that any ascent would take days. Then there was the complex history of the mountain that included fine climbers like the Victorian pioneer Mummery and the Tyrolese Reinhold Messner, and also included a black side just before the Second World War when many German climbers tried to make a first ascent for Hitler and place the swastika on the summit. As these thoughts, and many more, competed for my attention, I just stood before this great mountain in silent admiration and wonder.

On another occasion I was spellbound as the ice reflected a hundred or more different hues of blue and green from surreally sculptured ice walls on the Credner Glacier as we ascended Africa's highest mountain, Kilimanjaro, by an unusual route on its north-west flank. Earlier, I had watched the sun break over the ridge ahead of us and turn this land-scape from an ethereal pre-dawn gloominess to one saturated with warm orange light. This was so far removed from the usual tourist track up the mountain that we had seen only one other person in the last four days and felt part of a very precious wilderness.

Similarly walking through the Caucasus in former Russia there were so few people in the mountains that I thought this must have been how the Alps were a hundred years or more ago. With a huge area to explore, you often felt there were whole tracts where no one had been before. High in the mountains there was a tremendous sense of space, freedom and, on occasions, of silence.

These are all, to a greater or lesser extent, exotic places that involve time as well as money to visit. But a number of other wilderness areas to explore are nearer Britain, and some of them are not at all obvious. If you thought of Ireland, for instance, as an area not well suited to wilderness walking, then you would be wrong. While nowhere in Ireland is that far from a road or habitation, the very lack of people and the quietness of most roads mean that the situation of mountain and lowland is unique and one that we do not have in Britain. Take, for example, Macgillycuddy's Reeks, which provide arguably not only the finest ridge walk in the country but also a wilderness experience to compare with the very best. Although Ireland suffered from a series of famines and emigration that depleted the size of the population by a third, you still have habitations right up to the foot of the mountains. But once you start to gain height the picture changes dramatically and you can walk from one end of the Reeks to the other and see either no one or just a handful of fellow-walkers.

The traverse is usually done from east to west and although the distance is approximately eleven miles (eighteen kilometres) this is a tough walk involving 6000 feet (1830 m) of ascent and including six peaks of over that magical 3000-feet (914-m) mark (although let's have no mention of Irish Munros, please!). Depending on exactly which peaks you take in and how many diversions you make, this walk will take two or three days. There are many superb wild campsites although you may have to lose a little height to be near running water.

In my opinion, a number of factors serve to make this walk a memorable experience. While access to this part of Ireland is relatively easy and inexpensive (at the time of writing some flights to Cork via Dublin are a bargain), the place is culturally quite different to Britain. It may sound a cliché, but you could spend all your time just chatting to people and never reach the mountains! This would be a pity, because it's the physical form of these hills, which was caused mainly by the effects of glaciation, that brings back the faithful few year after year. Perhaps the best solution is to talk to the local people, many of whom have a wealth of knowledge about this landscape, *and* climb the hills! One writer has called this the most Irish of all walks, although it's almost impossible to say why: it is far easier once you are there as you look out across a landscape wrapped delicately in mist, look out over large areas of bog and take in, well, the Irishness of it all.

The classic traverse starts at Kate Kearney's Cottage (which is now a pub, a café and gift shop) west of Killarney and should end at The Climber's Inn at Glencar. The latter is on the road south-west of Lough Acoose and is marked on the Irish OS map as a post office and information centre. Both of these are true, but it's the beer and crack (friendly chat) that counts and, when you are in, say hello to Johnny and Anne for me.

They are the most hospitable of hosts and also offer accommodation, so there is no need to worry about getting home – at least not yet. As you sit in front of their peat fire and wonder exactly why they have a pulpit in the middle of the snug, you will be savouring memories of a quite outstanding trek.

What makes this traverse a classic outing is its sheer variety: even the plod across the moor to the first summit of Cnoc an Bhráca (2398 feet/731 m) gives a sense of space and isolation. There are superb views down to Lough an Chaca on the way to Cruach Mhór (3058 feet/932 m), after which the ridge becomes a jagged knife-edge taking in the Big Gun (3081 feet/939 m) on the way to Cnoc na Péiste (3241 feet/ 988 m), which is named after the lake below Lough Cummeenapeasta, or 'coomb of the serpent' where there is still a wing from an American plane that crashed here in the Second World War.

The ridge takes you unerringly onwards with ascents of Cnoc an Chuillinn (3143 feet/958 m) and Cnoc na Toinne (2772 feet/845 m) before descending to the saddle above the Devil's Ladder. This is a popular but eroded track up for day-walkers who join our route for the ascent of Ireland's highest mountain Carrauntoohil. Before starting the slog upwards on the scree, it is worth pausing to look down into the Hags Glen and the two lakes it contains. Throughout the whole of this ridge walk the effects of glaciation are seen easily, with high lake-filled corries and steep slopes carved out by the moving ice. In autumn the colours are superb, with a rich luminous green caused by a combination of temperate climate and abundant rainfall.

People often say that on a clear day standing on the summit of Carrauntoohil, at 3409 feet (1039 m), they feel that Ireland is spread out at their feet. I share this feeling, but I have been on the summit both in clear visibility and in thick mist and feel that this few feet of earth and rock has a presence all its own. Visitors from outside Ireland may be surprised by the large iron cross that dominates the top, but we should perhaps remember that we are, indeed, simply passers-by and accept that this religious symbol was placed here by the community within whose parish Carrauntoohil stands. However, I would not grieve too much if it were ever blown down – although the solidity of its construction makes that unlikely.

I wondered, the first time I did this traverse, if the remainder of the walk would be an anticlimax, a slow, gradual coming back into this rural community. I could not have been more wrong. Caher, the final peak on the ridge, is only slightly less high (3284 feet/1001 m) and the airy walk to it gives an ever-changing perspective into Coomloughra Glen and the two loughs. One of the loughs has the same name as the glen; the other is Lough Eagher. At times it looks as if the sides of this high glen fall sheer for hundreds of feet; at other instances my eye was pulled to the ragged jumble of rocks on the route ahead.

Finally, and with great reluctance, I left the summit of Caher. On the way I had seen more than one brocken spectre – a phenomenon whereby the sun shining through precipitation projects your giant shadow on to the clouds below while a small rainbow creates a halo effect around the edge. Earlier, I had watched as the sun broke through intermittent rain in great, bold shafts and, in the far south-west, had watched the late-afternoon light reflect off a distant lake to give an ethereal appearance to a darkening and mist-laden landscape. No walker ever wants to leave such a magical place as this.

As I walked off down a long glacial moraine, I looked across Dingle Bay and west-wards to the breakers of the Atlantic and northwards to that fine swath of peaks, including Brandon. Like many long walks, this one will leave a lasting impression, but what is it that so attracts me to such areas year after year?

Perhaps it is what the great American mountaineer Charles Houston once described as 'the joy of the journey'. Perhaps it is also the friendships we make along the way. And it is also undoubtedly a series of landscapes that can move all but the hardest soul.

Recently I was chatting to Hamish Brown, who for years has been championing the joys of another fine wilderness area – Morocco. As the conversation ebbed and flowed, what became clear was Hamish's unabashed enthusiasm for a landscape and people he had come to admire. He spoke about a traverse he and a party had just undertaken in the Atlas Mountains, enthusing about peaks they had climbed and what plans they already had for the next trip. As we shared memories and swapped stories, it became clear to me that however much you come to know and love an area, there will always be still more left to explore.

Neither Cameron nor I could manage for long without our wilderness 'fix' away from all the paraphernalia of modern life. Whenever I set off, I am reminded of a book about the Canadian north woods (somewhere else still to explore!), *Cache Lake Country*, written by John J. Rowlands in the late 1940s. I know virtually nothing about the author apart from recognizing the voice of a kindred spirit. He begins his account of life in this wilderness in a simple yet profound way that has stayed with me for many, many years. If anything can explain the attraction of the wilderness, these words can:

> *On most maps Cache Lake is only a speck hidden among other blue patches big enough to have names, and unless you know where to look you will never find it. But a place like Cache Lake is seldom discovered on a map. You just come on it – that is, if you are lucky. Most men who travel the north woods sooner or later happen on a lake or stream that somehow they cannot forget and always want to go back to. Generally they never do go back.*
>
> *Cache Lake lies deep in a wilderness of spruce and pine which, except for a timber cruiser like myself and maybe a trapper now and then, few white men know. So like many other worthwhile things, there's no easy trail to Cache Lake, for it is protected by distance, mile after forgotten mile of woods and water, and it is still clean and clear and safe from civilization.*

Index

Further Reading

Scottish Mountaineering Club and Scottish Mountaineering Trust publications
Donald Bennet, *The Munros*, 1985
Donald Bennet, *The Western Highlands*, 1983
D.J. Bennet and T. Strang, *The Northwest Highlands*, 1990
J.C. Donaldson, *Munro's Tables*, revised 1984
Peter Drummond, *Scottish Hill and Mountain Names*, 1991
D.J. Fabian, G. E. Little and D. N. Williams, *The Islands of Scotland including Skye*, 1989
Peter Hodgkiss, *The Central Highlands*, 1984
Scott Johnstone, Hamish Brown and Donald Bennet, *The Corbetts and other Scottish Hills*, 1993
Malcolm Slesser, *The Island of Skye*, 1981
Tom Strang, *The Northern Highlands*, 1982
Adam Watson, *The Cairngorms*, 1982

Other Publications
Hamish Brown, *Hamish's Mountain Walk*, Victor Gollancz 1978
Derek Cooper, *Skye*, Birlinn 1995

David Craig, *Landmarks*, Jonathan Cape 1995
David Craig, *Native Stones*, Secker & Warburg 1987
David Craig, *On the Crofters' Trail*, Jonathan Cape 1990
Paddy Dillon, *The Mountains of Ireland*, Cicerone Press 1992
Colin Fletcher, *The Complete Walker*, Alfred Knopf 1984
Seton Gordon, *Highways and Byways in the Central Highlands*, first published by Macmillan 1935
Seton Gordon, *Highways and Byways in the West Highlands*, first published by Macmillan 1935
Heading for the Scottish Hills, the Mountaineering Council of Scotland and the Scottish Landowners' Federation 1988
Ben Humble, *The Cuillin of Skye*, first published 1952, reprinted by The Ernest Press 1986
Archie MacDougall, *Knoydart – The Last Scottish Land Raid*, Lyndhurst Publications 1983
Osgood Mackenzie, *A Hundred Years in the Highlands*, The National Trust for Scotland 1921, revised edition 1949

P.A. Macnab, *Mull and Iona*, David and Charles, second revised edition 1987
Cameron McNeish, *The Munro Almanac*, Lochar Publishing 1991
Duncan M. MacQuarrie, *The Place Names of Mull*, John G. Eccles, Inverness 1982
W.H. Murray, *The Companion Guide to the West Highlands of Scotland*, Collins 1968
The Outer Hebrides Handbook and Guide, various local writers, Kittiwake Press 1995
John J. Rowlands, *Cache Lake Country*, A. & C. Blake 1948
Nan Shepherd, *The Living Mountain*, Aberdeen University Press 1977
Alexander Smith, *A Summer in Skye*, first published 1865, reprinted by Birlinn 1995
Seán ó Súilleabháin, *Southwest of Ireland*, Gill & Macmillan 1978
Francis Thompson, Harris and Lewis, *Outer Hebrides*, David and Charles, third revised edition 1987